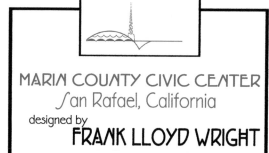

MARIN COUNTY CIVIC CENTER
ʃan Rafael, California
designed by
FRANK LLOYD WRIGHT
DOCENT TOUR

MARIN COUNTY CIVIC CENTER
ʃan Rafael, California
designed by
FRANK LLOYD WRIGHT
DOCENT TOUR

22 September 2004.

"Architectural features of true democratic ground-freedom would rise naturally from topography, which means that buildings would all take on the nature and character of the ground on which in endless variety they would stand and be component part."

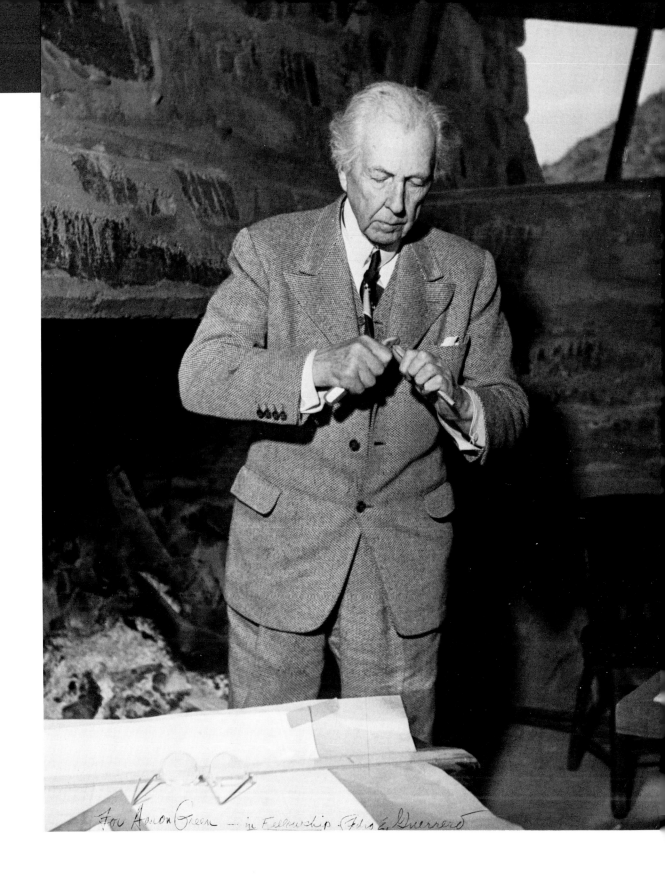

For Aaron Green — in Fellowship Pedro E. Guerrero

AN ARCHITECTURE FOR DEMOCRACY

FRANK LLOYD WRIGHT

THE MARIN COUNTY CIVIC CENTER

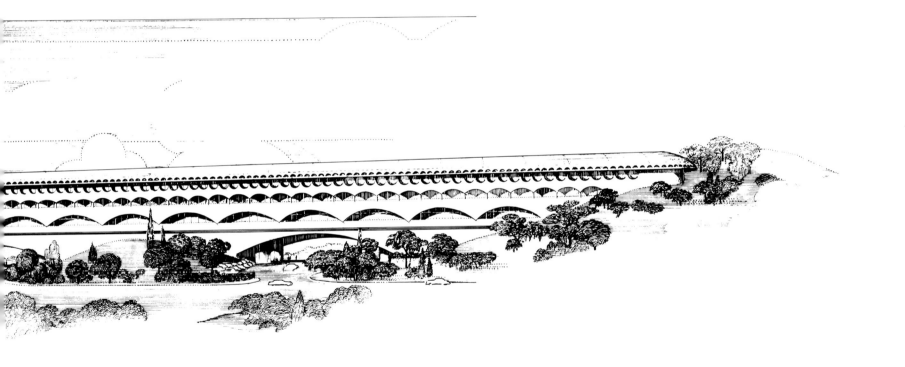

A NARRATIVE BY THE ASSOCIATED ARCHITECT
AARON G. GREEN, F.A.I.A.

WITH DONALD P. DE NEVI

MARIN COUNTY
ADMINISTRATION BUILDING
DEDICATED OCTOBER 13 1962

BOARD OF SUPERVISORS

WALTER R CASTRO	1950-
WILLIAM D FUSSELMAN	1942-
PETER H BEHR	1961-
GEORGE H LUDY	1961-
WILLIAM A GNOSS	1952-
VERA L SCHULTZ	1953-61
JAMES A MARSHALL	1955-61
J WALTER BLAIR	1961-61
JAMES V KEHOE	1941-55
WILLIAM Q WRIGHT JR	1952-55

CONTRACTOR
ROTHSCHILD RAFFIN AND WEIRICK INC

FRANK LLOYD WRIGHT
ARCHITECT

THE FRANK LLOYD WRIGHT FOUNDATION
TALIESIN ASSOCIATED ARCHITECTS
WILLIAM WESLEY PETERS CHIEF ARCHITECT
AARON G GREEN AIA
ARCHITECT ASSOCIATED

DEDICATION

This book is dedicated to two lovely and courageous ladies, Vera Schultz and the late Mary Summers. They were the catalysts and leaders in selecting Frank Lloyd Wright as architect for the Marin County Civic Center. To them we are all indebted.

Edited by Ben Raeburn and Nancy Klein.
Designed by Allan Wright Green
Typesetting by Archetype Visual Imaging Services, San Francisco
Printed by Walsworth Press, Marceline, Missouri

Orders should be addressed to:
    Grendon Publishing
    5 Third Street, Suite 224
    San Francisco, California 94103
    Telephone: (415) 777-0530
    FAX: (415) 777-1014

90 89 88 87 86 85 6 5 4 3 2 1

Library of Congress Catologing in Publication Data

Green, Aaron G. and DeNevi, Donald P.

Frank Lloyd Wright, An Architecture for Democracy,
The Marin County Civic Center, A Narrative by the Associated Architect.

1. Wright, Frank Lloyd, 1867-1959 — Interpretation and Appreciation
2. Architecture and Government — California
3. Organic Architecture — California
4. Architecture Modern — 20th Century — California
I. Wright, Frank Lloyd, 1867-1959
II. Green, Aaron and DeNevi, Donald
III. Title

Library of Congress Catalog Number: 89-81878

ISBN 0-9625029-0-1 (cloth)

ISBN 0-9625029-1-X (paper)

Contents

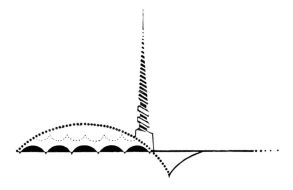

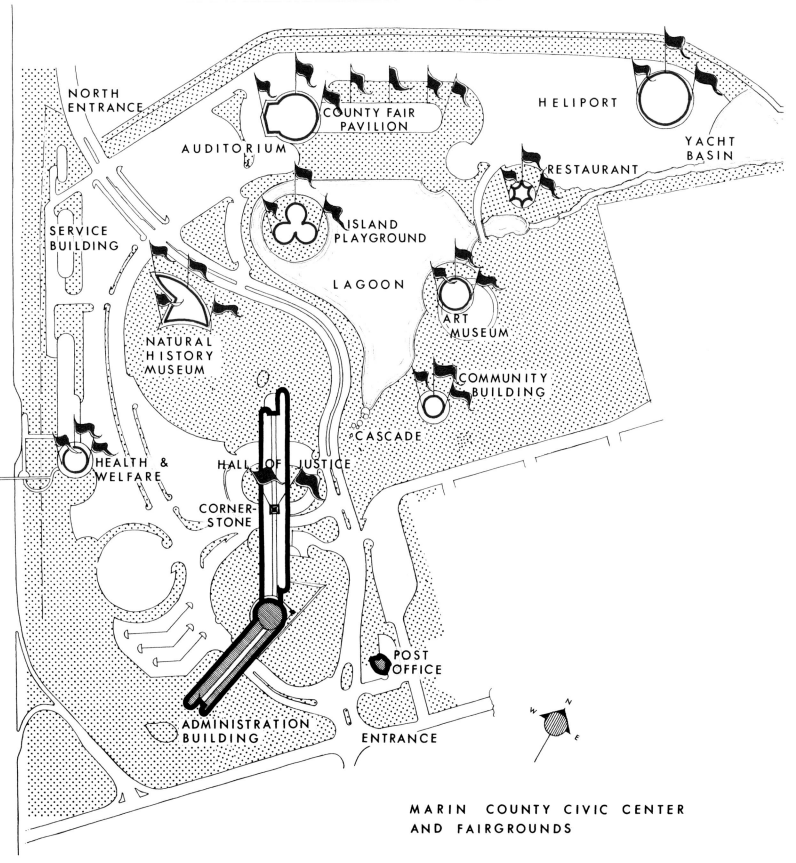

NORTH ENTRANCE

COUNTY FAIR PAVILION

HELIPORT

AUDITORIUM

YACHT BASIN

SERVICE BUILDING

ISLAND PLAYGROUND

RESTAURANT

LAGOON

NATURAL HISTORY MUSEUM

ART MUSEUM

COMMUNITY BUILDING

HEALTH & WELFARE

HALL OF JUSTICE

CASCADE

CORNER-STONE

POST OFFICE

ADMINISTRATION BUILDING

ENTRANCE

MARIN COUNTY CIVIC CENTER AND FAIRGROUNDS

Schematic master plan from program of ground breaking ceremony,
Hall of Justice.

ACKNOWLEDGEMENTS

Without the help and encouragement of many individuals, this book would not exist. My sincerest appreciation and thanks to: Renate Wunschkowski, my secretary, for her indefatigable assistance with many typed drafts and computer printouts; Allan Wright Green, for his book design; Donald DeNevi, coauthor, for his expert research and writing ability; Jan Novie, staff associate, for his general assistance and photography; Nancy Klein, for her coordinating and editing; Ben Raeburn, longtime friend of Frank Lloyd Wright and Horizon Press publisher of many fine Frank Lloyd Wright books, for his important consulting advice and editing; Marjorie Stengel, for her valuable help. Vera Schultz, Jim Haig, Lucille Dandelet, Marcelle McCoy Holck, and Allan Temko have also helped with suggestions for the text.

To the photographers who participated in the competition, "Focus on Frank Lloyd Wright," sponsored by Marin County and Adolph Gasser Company, thanks for the opportunity to select from your work for inclusion in the book; to Jay Silverberg, managing editor of the *Independent Journal*, thanks for use of your excellent photographs; and to Bruce Brooks Pfeiffer, archivist of the Frank Lloyd Wright Foundation, thanks for your assistance in making graphic material available.

FRANK LLOYD WRIGHT

AARON G. GREEN, A. I. A
SAN FRANCISCO REPRESENTATIVE
319 GRANT AVE. : YUKON 2-5149

PREFACE

It was a time when serious demographic changes in Marin County were accompanied by a new environmental sensitivity. There was fear that greed in development could undermine the quality of life, so much so, that a militant determination had risen to prevent destructive change. I was privileged to be introduced to that fascinating period.

It was a time of widening enlightenment. Civil rights were in a nascent stirring position, and so was the growing status of women who were inspiring social and political development in Marin County. It was a time of hope, destined to provide important historical sequences in an unfolding drama relating to the county's new government center for which I would be Frank Lloyd Wright's associated architect. From the beginning, every episode of this project was dramatic.

In 1957 my professional architectural work was just becoming involved with Marin County. In addition to residential work, I had been commissioned by the Marin County Housing Authority to design a new federal housing project at Marin City to replace a blighted wartime workers' housing area which had become a suburban slum. Just prior to the government center, this was the largest building project in the county. In that respect, I first met Mary Summers, planning director for Marin County. Her staff, under contract with Marin County's Housing Authority and Redevelopment Agency, had executed the master plan for the Marin City area. Mary Summers was a member of the county's committee to recommend an architect for its Civic Center. Frank Lloyd Wright was their selection. In addition to maintaining my own practice, I was Mr. Wright's West Coast representative. We had established a joint office in San Francisco in 1951.

A chaotic period was simmering in Marin County government. It was experiencing the last vestiges of cracker-barrel politics. A small clique of elected officials and appointed key staff who had been in charge for many years was sometimes referred to as the "courthouse gang." Population growth and an accelerating new constituency created a new look into basic constitutional rights and an interest in democratic participation.

In retrospect, it is significant to note that the major forces creating this memorable project were catalyzed and nurtured by several perceptive, strongly motivated women. A key turning point was the election of the county's first woman supervisor, Vera Schultz. University trained, qualified by her intellectual interest in honest government and idealistic concern for the growing role of women, Vera had an innate ability to get to the bottom of an issue and clarify it. Vera Schultz was the sparkplug in the Civic Center affair.

Mary Summers played a prominent role in decisive action. As director of planning for the county, she was not only the first woman county planning director, but one of the first in this new type of governmental position, destined to exercise a strong position in California's physical development. She was well suited to the task of saying no to the many pressures of those interested in expediency rather than quality concerning environmental issues. She hid an iron resolve behind a beguiling femininity and friendliness to see the job done properly. She and Vera Schultz quickly developed a team approach and were acknowledged leaders of the Marin County Board of Supervisors in the day-to-day decisions of developmental matters. But William D. Fusselman, the arch-conservative supervisor, opposed Vera Schultz on almost all issues in his last-ditch position against destruction of the old style politics of cronyism.

Mrs. Norman Livermore, one of Marin's most prominent philanthropists and a supporter of cultural development and environmental action, took the decisive lead in obtaining support to acquire the 145-acre site for dual use by the county and state-financed County Fair. The implications of joining cultural and recreational aspects of community life with government activities were setting the stage perfectly for application of the philosophy of Frank Lloyd Wright: "architecture for democracy."

Another who achieved a superb role in the developing drama of the Civic Center project was Walter Castro, the much loved "diamond in the rough" county supervisor. As chairman of the board, he was the official leader when Frank Lloyd Wright was commissioned architect. Walter was instinctively on the side of good and progress. Although educated by life and business experience, rather than by cultural conditioning, he became an ally and confidant of the leading ladies.

William Gnoss, similarly of fine political instincts for fair, honest government, passively joined the progressive majority in almost all voting and was dedicated to the Frank Lloyd Wright decision. William Gnoss was the only male supervisor who participated during the full episode spanning the origin and construction of the Frank Lloyd Wright Civic Center, and still lives to enjoy the fruits of his decisions. Supervisor James Marshall also voted with the progressive majority, favoring Frank Lloyd Wright's project.

It was a sense of the unique, dramatic impact of this building complex on the community, the realization that it was an enduring example of Frank Lloyd Wright's principles in building for democracy which prompted me to develop this book. There were also the many years of urging by my friend and fellow author, Donald DeNevi.

It is important to recognize the efforts of many officials of Marin County whose support made the project possible. Those who stand out in my mind from that crucial period are: Donald Jensen, first county administrator, and his successor, Alan Bruce; Lee Jordan, county counsel; Michael Mitchell, auditor and successor to Leon De Lisle; Donald Frost, director of the Department of Public Works and Arthur Knutson, assistant director; Les Wider, maintenance superintendent; Marcelle McCoy Holck, director of the County Fair; Honorable Peter Allen Smith and Honorable Warren McGuire from the judiciary. In later years, the efforts of County Counsel Douglas Maloney and County Administrator Thomas Campanella were important influences. Supervisor Al Aramburu has extended very special effort to encourage a heightened sensitivity and pride in the legacy of Frank Lloyd Wright.

Although this narrative is a first-person account by the associated architect, in no way is it intended to minimize the scope and effectiveness of the Frank Lloyd Wright Foundation architects under Wesley Peters' leadership. They participated at all times in all major decisions. Their work in developing the construction drawings was an admirable dedicated effort to carry on Frank Lloyd Wright's designs as he would have intended.

I will forever be grateful to the citizens of Marin County who possessed the foresight and courage to insist on the best standards in architecture as well as in government.

–Aaron G. Green, F.A.I.A.

FOREWORD

This book recaptures in fascinating detail how the Frank Lloyd Wright Civic Center became a reality. It tells the story, building by building, of the problems solved, the constraints overcome, the individuals engaged in causing the roadblocks or helping to resolve them.

As clients of an architect, none can be so feisty and unpredictable as government. Elected officials change, caution abounds, and the result is that most governmental architecture is drab, repetitive, and sterile.

The magic of the Marin County Civic Center came from the concept of a world-recognized genius, Frank Lloyd Wright, but Aaron Green's book recounts the struggle to move the concept to reality. And he is the best one to describe it, being Mr. Wright's associated architect, the one on location who had both the duty and the intense desire to complete the Center as a memorial to his mentor.

He spreads the credit around and leaves little for himself. In the difficult process of constructing the Administration Building, the Hall of Justice, and the Veterans Memorial Auditorium, Aaron played a leading role. He maintained his faith, his perseverance, and his patience throughout. And now we also learn he can write with clarity and conviction.

I worked as a county supervisor in the Administration Building for seven years, and give testimony to the pleasure of the experience. The Marin County Civic Center is truly described as "architecture for democracy."

— Hon. Peter H. Behr

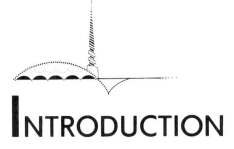

INTRODUCTION

Aaron Green's recollections of the creation of the Marin County Civic Center are pure gold to everyone who seeks the essence of Frank Lloyd Wright. The great autumnal commission for the only government buildings that Wright ever built summoned up a lifetime of faith in America's finer qualities, expressed in *An Architecture for Democracy* that was valiantly opposed to "Mobocracy," the destroyer of genius, which then lingered in Marin's cracker-barrel politics.

Aaron Green has recorded this devotion to excellence, maintained against considerable odds, which with fervor and humor prevailed in the unique monuments to the philosophy of Jefferson, Whitman, and, of course, Wright himself, which span the hills beside Highway 101 on the "graceful arches" Wright foresaw when he first visited the site.

The portrait of the Master in his last two years is indelible. Aaron Green has distilled his memories with the warmth expected in one of Wright's most gifted associates, and, in this case, as a full-fledged colleague, who on his own had enriched Marin County with low-cost housing that set a new standard for the country and is also architecture for democracy.

Yet the Wright depicted by Green, like Vasari's Michelangelo, is also a supreme artist who, to the end, sought new solutions to ever-evolving problems. The cable-supported tensile coverings of synthetic fabric which he proposed for the Marin Fairground, for instance, were fully a generation ahead of their time. This restless, innovative spirit was American in its finest details as well as in its limitless vision.

By its very nature, the vision can never be completely realized, but part of it came true in acrylic skylights and precast concrete, and even in the humane notion that prisoners could be helped back to useful civic life by magnificent views from a top-floor jail. Essential to all was the land, and Wright's refusal to bulldoze the hills, providing a lesson that Marin County still hasn't quite learned.

But the architecture is there as an education for us all, not least in democratic politics. The Master hoped that the buildings might last 300 years, and whatever else he taught us, we must hope with him.

—Allan Temko

CULTURAL CORNERSTONE

After only twenty minutes on the site, Frank Lloyd Wright decided on his design concept for the Marin County Civic Center. "I'll bridge these hills with graceful arches," he said to me as he described arcs in the air with his hands. That gesture seemed to conjure up his architecture as a reality.

We may now consider how his architecture exemplifies what he meant in a speech delivered the following year when he stated, "The good building is not one that hurts the landscape, but is one which makes the landscape more beautiful than it was before that building was built."

But this "cultural cornerstone," as he later termed it, did not develop without controversy, even a one-time threat of extinction. After construction was underway, a change in government immobilized the project with threats to turn it into a hospital. This created one of the most unique and dramatic democratic actions by citizens in American history. Purely in support of an architectural project, a citizens' revolt, including picketing of the county courthouse, demanded: "Save our Civic Center." As a consequence, the government was overturned. Never before had a county supervisor been recalled in California, as was the result in this case.

The entire Civic Center project was initiated by a phone call from Marin County Supervisor Vera Schultz to my San Francisco joint office with Frank Lloyd Wright. She said that a county committee was interviewing architects and asked whether there was any possibility that Frank Lloyd Wright might be available for consideration. I explained that I was willing to contact him about their commission only if they had concluded their interviews with other architects. I said it was my opinion that he would be receptive, and that they could discuss his services with me initially. However, he was not to be placed in competition with any other architects.

Later, I was contacted by Mary Summers for the architect search committee. She stated that the committee had concluded its interviewing and had decided its preference for Frank Lloyd Wright. I promptly notified him, and he agreed to a meeting.

In early July 1957, Mr. Wright was scheduled for a series of lectures at the University of California, Berkeley, and I was able to arrange the initial meeting in conjunction with that trip. The meeting was held in our San Francisco office with members of the search committee and the Marin Board of Supervisors minus one, William D. Fusselman, who had announced that he opposed the selection of Frank Lloyd Wright.

Aaron Green with Frank Lloyd Wright and helicopter rented to fly to San Francisco airport after his lecture series at University of California, Berkeley, July 1957.

The meeting was exploratory and cordial, with Mr. Wright typically relaxed, exhibiting all his natural poise and charm. He was asked about details of his services and how he would envision the project. In his characteristic manner, he expounded upon his theories and philosophy, especially in terms of an "architecture for democracy." He confirmed my previous advice that his fee would be ten percent of the construction cost.

After the meeting, as we walked from our office to the St. Francis Hotel, where he always preferred to stay, he remarked with pleasure that this commission would be his first civic structure. "Maybe we can show government how to operate better as a result of better architecture," he said.

Whenever he came to San Francisco, we always stopped by the V. C. Morris shop on Maiden Lane, the china and gift shop which he had designed in 1949. Upon entering, we were greeted enthusiastically by the owners, Mr. and Mrs. Morris, who were always mesmerized, but pleased, as they watched Frank Lloyd Wright rearrange the store's furniture and displays. He typically asked me to go out and buy flowers to enliven the place. Even though they loved him and the building, I knew that once we left, the Morrises would put everything back the way it was. Their merchandising was classic and ascetic, rather than emotional and colorful.

After a year-long search and interviews with twenty-six architects, the Marin County Board of Supervisors, on July 26, 1957, voted four to one officially to retain Mr. Wright. William Fusselman, who represented the arch-conservative constituency of the county, voted against the other four. He was inevitably against anything proposed by Vera Schultz.

The Civic Center site previously purchased was on the east side of Highway 101, some 300 yards north of the San Rafael city limits. The government portion of the site would be the southern section of the 145 acres. The Marin County Fairgrounds would occupy the northern section, and would also be part of the architects' commission.

After the committee vote, I flew to Taliesin West, Mr. Wright's headquarters in Arizona, to discuss the project. It was much too important for the usual telephone communication. I was naturally brimming with pride as I walked into Mr. Wright's office, announced the committee's decision, and said that the Marin County Board of Supervisors was ready to offer a contract. Mr. Wright smiled and said, "I will only accept the job with you as the associated architect on a fifty-fifty basis." After regaining my composure, I responded by asking how I could justify that privilege. He said, "You already have."

I had worked in the past on numerous projects with Frank Lloyd Wright but had always received my compensation from his clients, the standard arrangement for field supervisory services of a representative from his office. When I returned to San Francisco, I wrote Mr. Wright a letter stating, "I realize you said we would split the fee on a fifty-fifty basis, but I want you to know that as far as I'm concerned, you are free to change that in any way you wish. It's much too generous."

Subsequently, at one of our meetings at Taliesin, he commented, "We've talked about that fee business, and I suggest that instead of a fifty-fifty split of the net profit, we'll use a straight two-thirds, one-third, with our usual furnishing of drawings, engineering, etc. That way we'll avoid bookkeeping." The honor and privilege he was bestowing on me clearly flowed from his appreciation of my years of effort to bring him commissions, and my activities which succeeded in getting his projects constructed. By that time, I had in some manner participated in nearly thirty Frank Lloyd Wright projects. When I asked what he expected me to do for such a generous share, he said, "Just what you have been doing."

Later, as I thought about that brief exchange, I chuckled to myself. I doubted that he had talked to anyone about the fee arrangement except perhaps Mrs. Wright. He was not the sort of man who involved others in his decision making.

On July 30, 1957, Frank Lloyd Wright arrived in San Francisco to accept his 770th commission, the creation of a multimillion dollar Civic Center for Marin County. He was ninety years old. To his disappointment, he could not obtain a helicopter at the airport to fly over the bay to San Rafael, where he was to address a meeting of the Marin County officials. He told the newsmen at the arrival gate that he had no sketches or plans because he was just being hired. He explained, "I never design a building until I've seen the site and met the people who will be using it," and added that he was "happy to be striking a blow for quality."

On the evening of signing the contract, an overflow crowd of more than 500 people listened to his speech in the San Rafael High School Auditorium. He spoke casually to the audience. "The beauty of Marin County should be expressed in our architecture. The buildings must not hurt the land. I regard this as a real opportunity. Marin County has nearly everything. The buildings of the new Civic Center will express this natural beauty; they will not be a blemish upon the landscape." He congratulated the Board of Supervisors for choosing a rural site with adequate space so that the Center was not to be crowded. "My buildings," he said proudly, "will last at least 300 years." Mr. Wright then asked for questions from the audience. "I'm now part of your family and I want to know what you want in your Center." A young girl asked, "Are you going to knock down any hills?" "Not a single one," he smiled.

I was aware that opposition against Mr. Wright was mounting from the Marin Chapter of the American Legion and a conservative, reconstituted minority group calling themselves The Taxpayers Association. When we entered the Board of Supervisors' chambers for the official appointment of the architect, Mr. Wright was greeted by smiles and nods from all directions. The meeting started with the usual opening greeting and agenda, then promptly turned to the matter at hand, the official acceptance of the contract. At this point, just before the vote, County Clerk George Jones asked permission to read a letter into the record from a representative of the opposition group. That incredible letter stated that Mr. Wright had communist leanings and had been an antiwar activist! Sitting next to Mr. Wright, I saw his confused expression of disbelief. I had never seen him nonplussed by any situation before. I tugged on his arm and said, "Mr. Wright, you don't have to listen to this!" He jumped from his seat, as if catapulted, shouting untypically, "Aw, rats! Take me as I am or not at all." He moved his cane angrily as he paused at the auditorium's exit and shouted, "This is an absolute and utter insult, and I will not be subjected to it."

Frank Lloyd Wright had always been a strong antiwar pacifist. Although he had made a trip to Russia as a guest of their architects' organization, he always spoke of the great differences in our social systems and his preference for the democratic way of life. His main philosophical thesis had always been the preservation of individualism. Certainly he had no communist leanings. His patriotic love for America was unbounded, and among his heroes were the likes of Thomas Jefferson and Walt Whitman.

In the corridor, as we headed for the car, Mary Summers came running up behind us. She clung to his arm, saying, "Please Mr. Wright, this doesn't mean a thing. Those people don't represent county opinion, but the supervisors have no way of stopping them from speaking. So please don't take this seriously." The reassurances made him feel better. He said, "O.K., let's go see the site." When we arrived at the site, a jeep was waiting and Mr. Wright climbed into the front seat with Marvin Brigham, director of the Public Works Department, while Mary Summers and I got into the back.

As we rode over the hilly terrain, he was delighted. At one point, we got out, climbed through strands of a barbed-wire fence, and then walked through knee-high grass. From the top of one hill, seeing the entire property, he said, "It's as beautiful as California can have." He paused a few moments, then turned to me and without the slightest hesitation said, "I know exactly what I'm going to do here." Upon seeing the first rough sketch three months later, I realized that the solution was precisely as he had first visualized it.

Vera Schultz told reporters she felt the incident that morning was a carefully laid plot against Mr. Wright. She said that County Clerk Jones had failed to show up with the contract which Mr. Wright was to sign. No copies of the documents were to be found in Jones's office, and she believed Jones was on the side of the project's enemies who hoped to prevent Mr. Wright from signing until after the communist charges were read.

As it turned out, the Board of Supervisors' chairman, Walter Castro, had been warned and therefore had a carbon copy of the contract in his pocket at the auditorium, where Mr. Wright was to deliver his speech that evening. Mr. Wright put his signature to this and then told reporters that he defied anyone to show he was, or ever had been, a communist sympathizer. "There is no substance in that. I'm a loyal American. Look at my record! I challenge anyone to prove one act or one association which could be called subversive."

After the contract was signed, it was my responsibility to work with county officials to secure all backup information necessary to develop a program of design. I immediately began the task. It required more than three months. A year before, the county had retained an administrative consultant, familiar with municipal operations, whose job was to conduct an administrative and space analysis. With that report as reference, I assessed its every statement thoroughly and then interviewed every Marin County department head, every person in county government who could provide meaningful information. As a result of this effort, I developed a space program which varied considerably from the one which had been submitted by the administrative analyst. My studies revealed that much more space was required than had originally been considered. The previous analysis had underestimated space, cost, future requirements, virtually everything. Use of the facility for almost three decades confirmed the validity of my analysis, in contrast to the inadequate assessment by the administrative consultant. The analysis was for a projected space need of only twenty-five years, which at that time seemed a long period ahead.

View from east on a foggy morning

*"**A**gain in America we erect temples but this time not so much to the mystery of great terrestrial or cosmic forces as to the interior or spirit-power of manhood as released by American democracy and its sciences."*

Frank Lloyd Wright's quotations arranged adjacent to photographs of the Civic Center are verbatim quotations from his various writings.

View from west

View from east

*The colors of the building
merge with the colors of nature*

42

MARIN COUNTY FAIR A M P H I T H E A T E R
MARIN COUNTY GOVERNMENT CENTER
F R A N K L L O Y D W R I G H T A R C H I T E C T

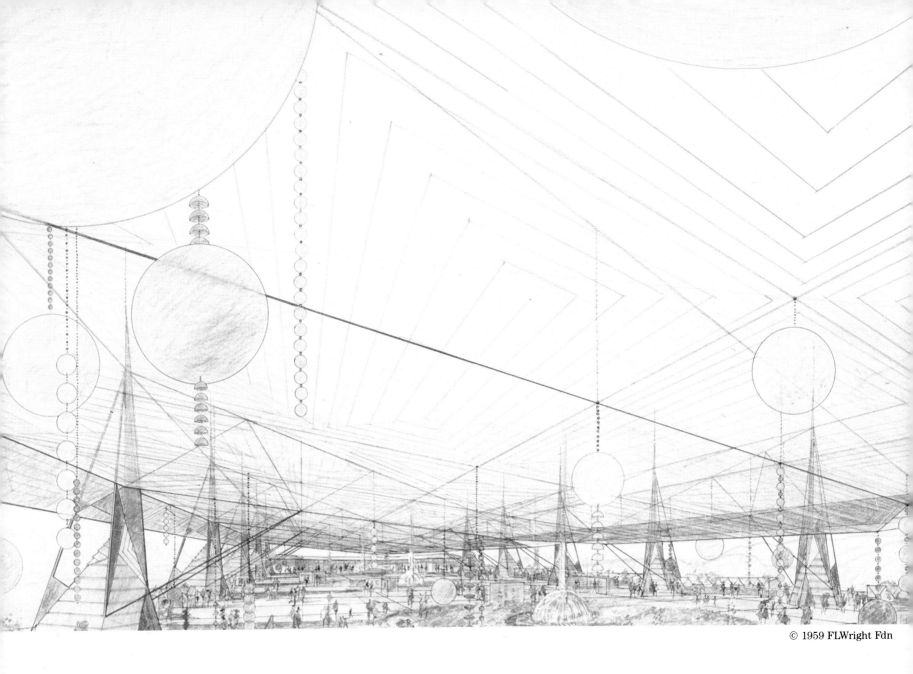

MARIN COUNTY FAIR

"The outside of any building may now come inside and the inside go outside, each seen as part of the other. Continuity, plasticity, and all the new simplicity they imply have at last come home."

Entrance gates

Ceramic tiles used as Frank Lloyd Wright's signature on his buildings were produced by Aaron Green and Jeanette Haber, his mother-in-law.

"*The sense of space within the reality of any building is a new concept wherever architecture is concerned. But it is essential ancient principle just the same and is not only necessary now but implied by the ideal of democracy itself.*"

"*Wherever human life is concerned, the unnatural stricture of excessive verticality cannot stand against more natural horizontality.*"

"Noble life demands a noble architecture for noble uses of noble men. Lack of culture means what it has always meant: ignoble civilization and therefore imminent downfall."

"The dynamic ideal we call democracy, gradually growing up in the human heart for two thousand five hundred years, at least, has now every opportunity to found the natural democratic state in these United States of America by way of natural economic order and a natural, or organic, architecture."

"Organic architecture is the only true architecture for our democracy. Democracy will some day realize that life is itself architecture organic, or else both architecture and mankind will become in vain together."

"*N*ow *because the American citizen will learn how expanded light, spacious openness and firm cleanliness of significant line in oneness of the whole may be his own, and how all may add to his stature as a man among men, he will not be stampeded.*"

60

"Beautiful buildings are more than scientific. They are true organisms, spiritually conceived; works of art, using the best technology by inspiration rather than the idiosyncrasies of mere taste or any averaging by the committee mind."

CREATION

Mr. Wright, demonstrating great enthusiasm for the project, began working immediately. Several weeks after I forwarded the space program to him, I received his telephone call requesting that I fly to Taliesin West, "to see what we have done." Strangely enough, this great genius, considered egocentric by many, often used the "we" pronoun.

In the early days, there was no telephone at Taliesin West. I had to send wires which were picked up at Paradise Inn in Scottsdale, Arizona, six miles away. Often my telegrams stated, "Please contact me," and Mr. Wright would respond by telephoning me when he went to town. I always preferred an opportunity to talk with him directly, rather than communicate by correspondence, which in retrospect, rendered my archival records of our association much more sparse than if more had been documented in writing. When a radio telephone was installed at Taliesin, our inability to communicate directly was worse than ever. In order to communicate with him, one had to talk through the radio telephone operator. I would explain something to the operator who would then try to convey the message to Mr. Wright. She would often get its essence garbled. Inevitably misunderstandings resulted.

When I flew to Taliesin the first time after the contract had been signed, I saw the "graceful arches" he had orginally described at the site. Everything he envisioned was there. Mr. Wright explained the salient points of his scheme, the relationship to site, and the effectiveness of multiple entrances from parking areas. He was particularly proud of the interior central mall between two office bays, which he said would allow for natural air conditioning and natural lighting. The symphony of arches was his basic inspiration. As the conversation ended, he said, "Now you can take the drawings and do whatever you want with the interior. You wanted it flexible." He referred to the space analysis I had provided.

In short, he had successfully designed a functional structure which would easily adapt to a flexible arrangement of interior partitions. He wasn't interested specifically to lay out the inside partitions at that time, because the geometry of interior spaces of each departmental area would be temporary. A great flexibility was perhaps his major contribution to the functional aspects of the design. Today, twenty-eight years later, the many modifications of interior partitions, which occurred to accommodate changing needs, dramatically demonstrated the validity of Frank Lloyd Wright's design concept.

On Tuesday, March 25, 1958, Frank Lloyd Wright arrived in San Francisco

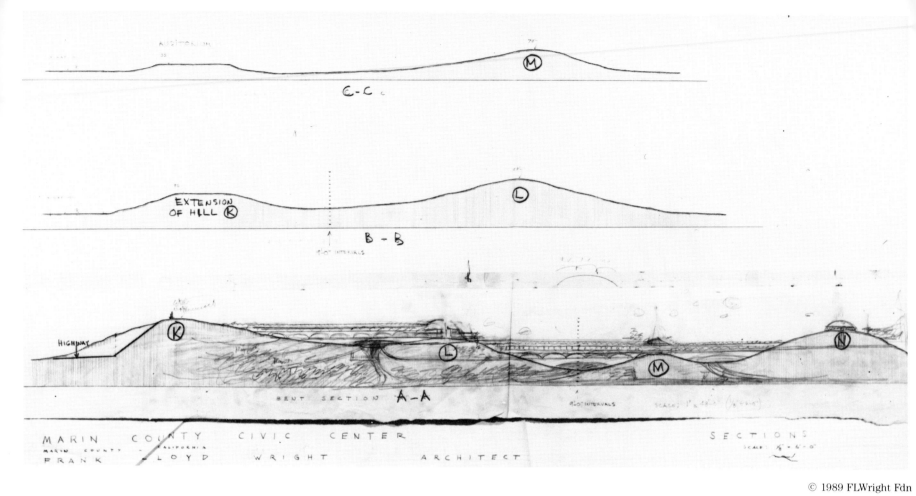

Full Elevation and Siting

Frank Lloyd Wright's first design sketches, never before published.

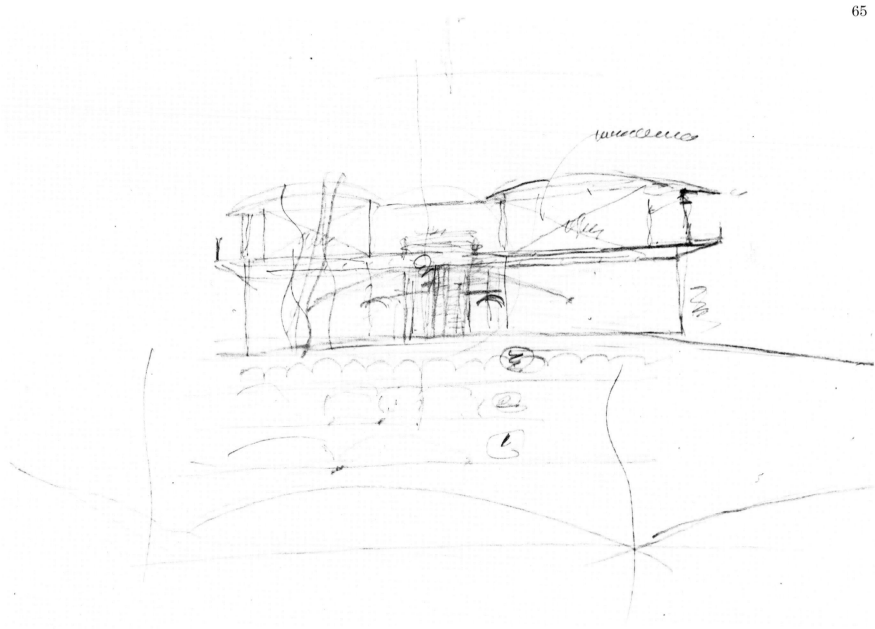

Cross Section and Elevation

with his finished, radiantly colored drawings. They had typically been executed by members of the Taliesin staff under his supervision, but showed a greater than usual amount of attention. The beautiful renderings were by exceptionally competent staff members John Howe and Ling Po, but also revealed much of Mr. Wright's own handiwork.

Along with the drawings, Mr. Wright presented cost estimates, which Wesley Peters and I had assembled over a long sleepless weekend. The drawings and cost estimates had been compiled in less than three months from the time I had seen the first sketch.

The following afternoon, more than 700 Marin residents jammed the San Rafael High School auditorium to hear Mr. Wright discuss his plans for the new Civic Center. The drawings were displayed across the street in the school's cafeteria. With the auditorium packed to overflowing, Mr. Wright began his speech. After a few sentences he started to describe the basis for his designs. Suddenly, he stopped in mid-sentence and asked, "You have all seen the drawings, haven't you?" When the audience responded in chorus, "No," he smiled and said, "All right, then let's all go over right now and see the drawings." Whereupon he stopped his speech. Everyone in the audience exited from the auditorium and walked across the street to view the precious drawings displayed in the cafeteria. All 700 people then walked back to the auditorium where he continued his speech.

It was certainly an historic occasion. The unpredictable spontaneity and informality were characteristic of Frank Lloyd Wright. He then went on to describe his design: "So flexible and simple as to be almost unbelievable. The overall result will be a cornerstone in the culture of the nation, and all the structures will melt into the sunburnt hills. My designs are in great conformance with the beautiful nature of Marin. Instead of slicing away the hills with bulldozers," he said, "the buildings will bridge the knolls with graceful arches." He explained the concept of pendant crescents, nonstructural scalloped arches suspended across the front of the structure to shield the glass facade from the sun. "Eventually, the long three-story steel and concrete structure will house all the county offices currently in the old courthouse. Appended is a tall, slender radio and television tower as a vertical accent and identifying feature. I have used the concrete and steel of modern technology, making possible a substantial economy."

The larger wing would be built in phase two, to be completed in 1969, and house the courts, law enforcement offices, and the county jail. Upon completion, Marin would also have a fairground with a lagoon, an element of beauty as well as part of a drainage system. He concluded his presentation by saying, "It is a terrific thing to get a building built that has the qualities of greatness in it."

In the weeks that followed, I assisted a small active group of citizens, headed by Harold Stockstad and county officials, particularly Mary Summers, in establishing an educational program. It was desirable to raise Marin residents' awareness to the significance of organic architecture. Stockstad led in producing an excellent film strip entitled "Marin's Finest Hour." With full-size reproductions of the architectural plans and colored renderings, this formed an exhibition which traveled throughout the county via bookmobile. Accompanied by dedicated citizens to answer questions, this grass roots educational effort was very effective in stimulating enthusiasm and support for the project.

On April 28, 1958, Frank Lloyd Wright's plan for the Marin County Civic Center received the official go-ahead from the county Board of Supervisors amid great applause from another overflow audience at a public hearing in the San Rafael Courthouse. The vote was four to one with Fusselman again demanding that the whole idea be submitted to a vote by the people. It turned out, however, that a large, appreciative number spoke in favor of the plan. Dr. S. I. Hayakawa, then San Francisco State College Professor of Semantics, said, "The plans do contain the correlation of spirit with the surrounding scenery." A San Rafael architect announced that a little noted fact was that Mr. Wright's plan would save money. "It has an extremely simple layout. You couldn't ask for more economy."

Throughout the remainder of the year, the work on the construction drawings proceeded at Taliesin. I continued to provide detailed layouts for the building's interiors, acting as liaison with the client and our local technical consultants, while the Taliesin staff worked on the construction drawings under Mr. Wright's direct supervision.

LANDSCAPE DESIGN

Having previously been responsible for several Frank Lloyd Wright landscape design projects, I was assigned to handle the Civic Center's landscape design as well. Mr. Wright was intensely interested in plant materials and their adaptability to the specific environmental conditions of each project. Because of his farming background, he had an innate sense of the use of plant materials. His concepts were always informal, making transitions between the manmade aspects of the building and the natural forms of the environment.

When driving around the Bay Area, Mr. Wright observed the prevailing use of plants in the landscape and often discussed the desirability for specific plants. One of his favorites was the deodar cedar. He was enamored of the graceful, pendant branch shapes and hoped to incorporate the deodar cedar into the Civic Center landscape design. I wasn't sure whether this tall, lush, blue-green tree would do well at that site, but he loved it.

Because the overall site was barren of trees except for a few characteristic oaks, I suggested advance planting in those areas which did not directly adjoin the construction area. Mary Summers, director of the Planning Department who was also a landscape architect, provided a list of potential plant materials which the county could obtain free for the advanced planting. Considering ways by which this could be done inexpensively, we discussed employing inmate labor from the county jail. We also considered employing Boy Scouts, but the advance planting project never developed beyond some trees which the Scouts did plant. Unfortunately, the Scouts who volunteered to water the trees had a picnic in the area and accidentally started a fire that burned down the trees they had planted.

Mary Summers was familiar with plant materials in the local area and became a consultant upon whom we could depend. Because of the broad scope of the project and a concern for economy of maintenance, I also developed a consulting relationship with the director of the State Division of Highways Landscape Department, Dana Bowers, and his assistant, Jim Gordon. Plans and specifications for all designs were submitted to them for review to ensure that everything was technically best for the local climate and the environment of the Civic Center project.

The deodar trees that Mr. Wright loved so much were among the few things that unfortunately did not work well in the landscape scheme.

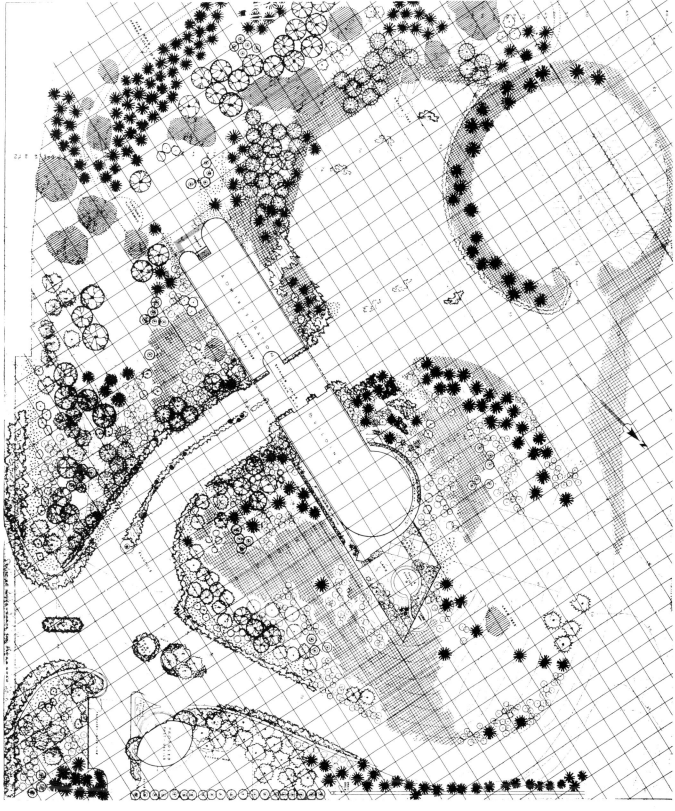

M A R I N   C O U N T Y   G O V E R N M E N T   C E N T E R
ADMINISTRATION BUILDING   MARIN COUNTY CALIFORNIA
F R A N K   L L O Y D   W R I G H T   A R C H I T E C T

L A N D S C A P E   P L A N
SCALE 1"=30'0"   UNITS 32'0"x 32'0"
0' 15' 30'   60'   120'   240'

TALIESIN ASSOCIATED ARCHITECTS
THE FRANK LLOYD WRIGHT FOUNDATION   SEPTEMBER 10, 1959
S H E E T   S D   2

On April 9, 1959, at 4:30 a.m., at the age of 92, Frank Lloyd Wright died. Marin County was to have his last major design project.

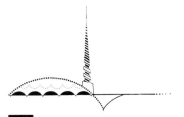

THE FUTURE AT STAKE

After telegraphing their sympathy to Mrs. Wright, county officials announced that the contract to design the Civic Center had been made with the Frank Lloyd Wright Foundation, not with Mr. Wright personally, which allowed it to continue. All of the important design work on the plans had been finished by Mr. Wright for the first and second stages. Supervisor Vera Schultz said, "We have felt his genius in the designs and we will certainly go through with them. Mr. Green and the Taliesin staff, as architects and engineers, can carry them on." I made several telephone calls to give my professional guarantee that a satisfactory continuation would be maintained by a combination of my efforts and those of the Taliesin group.

As a result of Mr. Wright's death, more responsibility fell on my shoulders. Taliesin Senior Architect William Wesley Peters and I formed a closely knit team. Our cooperative effort became highly efficient. The personnel of Frank Lloyd Wright's seasoned and capable staff, now formed as Taliesin Associated Architects, assiduously applied their efforts to the completion of the drawings. They included chief draftsman John Howe, John deKoven Hill, John Rattenbury, Tom Casey, and Kenn Lockhart. All of them, except John Howe who later came to join my organization, are still leaders in the work at Taliesin.

I was delegated the responsibility for interior layouts, cabinetwork, site development, landscape, and specifications in addition to my usual local liaison and construction administration. Had Frank Lloyd Wright lived, almost all of this work would have emanated directly from his hand and his supervision at Taliesin. Now we had to accomplish it cooperatively in the manner we had been trained to do, and as closely as possible to how we believed Mr. Wright would have done it. It was an intense and dedicated labor of love and unrestricted effort. Our responsibility to Frank Lloyd Wright weighed heavily, and the future was at stake.

Near the end of the construction document development, several of the Taliesin architects brought their pencils to the San Francisco office. Working together, often into the wee hours of night, we finalized all the drawings and specifications within our target schedule. It was truly a cooperative achievement. Next came the bidding process. Although often stressful, in this case, surprisingly it was not. The lowest bid was below the target estimates. Shortly thereafter, a contract was awarded to the well-established Bay Area firm, Rothschild, Raffin and Weirick, Inc.

THE FIRST BUILDING

The first building actually constructed on the Civic Center site was the Frank Lloyd Wright-designed post office. The United States Postal Service was interested in having a branch at that location, but the Marin County Board of Supervisors decided that the post office had to be designed by Frank Lloyd Wright and relate to his master plan or else they would not include it on the site. Such insistence was not customary in federal post office procedure for a branch post office. Typically, bidders provided their own design, following specifications by the government. The bidding was based upon the amount of rent to be charged to the government over a twenty-year lease period. The Board of Supervisors decided that if the post office was a design by Mr. Wright, they would consider leasing the site for one dollar a year over a period of fifty years. Such an idea would not have survived through the post office bureaucracy except for the creative energy and interest of one man, John Keast, who was in charge of the Post Office Department's regional real estate office. Mr. Wright's fee would be paid by the successful bidder who would agree to construct the building according to the architect's plans and specifications.

John and Evelyn McDonnell of Upper Darby, Pennsylvania, were the successful bidders. They were interested not only in the project as an investment, but also in the unique Frank Lloyd Wright design.

John McDonnell engaged me to handle the process of rebidding to local contractors who would build the post office for his account. Even though he was a general contractor, he did not want to operate from Philadelphia. Thus, the post office was successfully constructed, accepted, and became the first operational unit of the Civic Center. The dedication occurred before that of the Administration Building, which was then nearing completion. Today, in the post office lobby, there is a dedication plaque bearing the names of John Fitzgerald Kennedy and Frank Lloyd Wright.

One of the more interesting aspects of the post office design was a large plastic globe of the world at the entrance facade of the building. Half of the globe was on the exterior facade and half was on the inside of the lobby's glass front. My office donated the gold leaf painting of the world's continents on the globe's surface. Unfortunately, the globe was vandalized and the plastic cracked. The post office never replaced it. I have often thought that the county supervisors should pressure the Post Office Department to replace this extraordinary globe designed by Frank Lloyd Wright as an integral part of the building. The interest and integrity of the original design would then be maintained.

ADMINISTRATION BUILDING GROUND BREAKING

Nearly a year after Mr. Wright's death, the ground-breaking ceremony took place. On Monday, February 15, 1960, some 500 people, including his widow, Mrs. Olgivanna Lloyd Wright; Mr. Wright's eldest son, Architect Lloyd Wright; his grandson, Architect Eric Wright; and other dignitaries, attended the ceremonies marking the beginning construction of the Administration Building. Mrs. Wright spoke, "This historic moment proves that in a government by the people and for the people, we can have the finest in the world brought about by the citizens."

Distinguished Architect Edward Stone, in his address, stated, "It has been said that all great periods of history were great only because of the arts they produced. You people here in Marin County will have a great work of art, the best that our times can produce. I prophesy this will be a place of pilgrimage in years to come. They will come here as they go to see Michelangelo today."

STOP WORK

In spite of acceptance by virtually the entire Marin community, on Tuesday, January 11, 1961, after approximately one year into construction, a small group of Civic Center enemies incredibly brought the project to a halt. This occurred because in the June 1960 primary election, Supervisors Vera Schultz and Jim Marshall had been defeated for reelection by new aspirants Walter Blair and George Ludy. The election upset the previous balance of supervisory power, leaving Supervisors Walter Castro and William Gnoss as the pro-Civic Center minority.

A reassessment program for property taxes had first occurred in Vera Schultz's district. This infuriated many voters who incorrectly blamed Vera, although she actually had no control over the decision which reassessed her constituents' property first in the county. Fusselman was reelected. The Civic Center project had played a heavy part in the campaign, but that was not the issue which defeated the two incumbents, as was strongly demonstrated later.

As one of its first official actions, the new Board of Supervisors, by a three to two vote, ordered a work stoppage on the Administration Building. The construction was well out of the ground and some 125 workers were laid off the job. Fusselman, who spearheaded the revolt, said the temporary stop order was dictated by economic reasons. His plan was to convert the Civic Center into a county hospital facility. "This stoppage is going to reduce the impact on the taxpayers' pocketbooks," he insisted.

Nearly $1 million of work had already been done on the building. If the order became permanent, the contractors would hold the county liable for an unspecified amount of damages. It was obviously neither architecturally possible nor financially feasible to convert the building into a hospital.

The incredible stoppage caused an uproar. Marin County auditor, Leon De Lisle, a member of the Civic Center Committee, said, "I'm so mad I can't speak. Stopping the job last year would have been very expensive, but nothing compared to the cost of such a move now." State Senator John F. McCarthy, a Republican from San Rafael, added, "We in the legislature have authorized a state fund for a county fairground to be built on the Civic Center site, and there would be serious legal difficulty if everything were stopped. I hope the supervisors take a long look before doing this."

Fusselman was supported by his newly elected fellow board members, J. Walter Blair, a laundromat tycoon, and George Ludy, a grocer. Since Fusselman's profession was that of a candymaker, this occasioned a rather hilarious newspaper cartoon after the child's nursery rhyme, "Rub-a-Dub-Dub, Three Men in a Tub." Blair and Ludy, who had campaigned with a platform plank opposed to Mr. Wright's plan, claimed their election was a mandate against the project. Subsequent actions by the citizens proved that this was not the case.

The day after the irresponsible work stoppage order, a large number of angry Marin County residents bombarded a citizens advisory committee in San Rafael with protests. Known as the Citizens Advisory Committee for the Development of Marin County, the committee had been formed three years previously by the Board of Supervisors for slum clearance. The spokesman for the more than 200 fuming residents said, "This action is a subterfuge for the complete abandonment of the Civic Center, regardless of the consequences. This constitutes malfeasance on the supervisors' part." County Auditor Leon De Lisle charged that Fusselman and his two supporters had already begun weeding out committee leaders who favored the Civic Center. He said he was summarily fired from the committee by mail just the day before.

Under the leadership of Harold Stockstad, a civil engineer from Tamalpais Valley, a pro-Civic Center Committee was immediately formed. It vowed to fight for continuance to the bitter end of the Civic Center. Meanwhile, workers laid off were upset, claiming the work stoppage had created a pocket depression. Contractors and subcontractors threatened, if the nonsense continued, to sue the county and recover their investments.

Harold Stockstad was superbly effective as spokesman, and the democratic process of citizens' action developed a public protest demonstration at the county courthouse, including picketing. This was probably the first time in history that a citizens' democratic uprising developed over a building. Frank Lloyd Wright would have been proud!

The next day, Auditor Leon De Lisle announced publicly, to the delight of the committee and their supporters, that he would defy any attempt to shift the Center's funds to other uses. He told reporters, "Any money appropriation needs a yes vote by four of the five supervisors. Should I receive a demand to use the Civic Center's earmarked funds for something else, I will refuse payment and impound the funds until such time as they are appropriated for some other use, or for the Civic Center by a four-fifth vote of the board."

Many architectural professionals indicated support. President of the San Francisco American Institute of Architects, George Rockrise, made a personal appearance in support. Six Marin County architects fired off a letter to the Board of Supervisors saying that to shift the plans into something as highly specialized as a hospital would result in an extremely costly structure of makeshift design. Marin's newspaper, the *Independent Journal*, conducted a questionnaire poll which indicated support of the project by a majority of citizens.

The project architects were dumbfounded by the stop-work order, as was the contractor, but the political climate in the county demanded that they maintain a wait-and-see stance. I had to reply to many questions from various newspapers, county staff members, and interested citizens, and, of course, there were the usual behind-the-scenes telephone conversations relative to strategy. The Marin architectural firm of Crawford and Banning had been officially requested by the Board of Supervisors' majority to prepare a report concerning the feasibility of turning the building project into a hospital. This was such an outlandish notion that it was easy to deride with technical and cost information. I was certain that the reputable firm of architects chosen for the report would describe the hospital issue negatively. But there was no way to predict further action by the majority political faction which erroneously believed it had received a mandate at the voting booth to act against the project!

The *Independent Journal* poll showed that seven out of eight residents favored continuing the project. Another salutary factor was the report from the architectural firm officially commissioned by the Board of Supervisors which determined that the building could not practically be converted to another use. In addition, the county counsel informed the supervisors that cancellation of the original contract would result in damage claims of $2 million or more. On January 17, 1961, Fusselman's board threw in the towel in recognition of the citizens' anger. After the unsettling one-week work stoppage, the board voted unanimously to resume construction of the Civic Center immediately.

With the issue settled, lay members of the citizens committee, who spearheaded the drive for completion of the Center, met later that night to establish a permanent organization. The Council for Civic Responsibility was formed to scrutinize all county government operations in the future. "We are not completely at ease about the Board of Supervisors," said a committee spokesperson.

RECALL

As an aftermath of this dramatic episode, a recall movement was begun against one of the newly elected supervisors who had been particularly vocal against the project. For the first time in the history of California, a county supervisor was to be recalled. The recall election placed Peter Behr instead of Walter Blair in the position of supervisor. From that time on, the political climate of the Board of Supervisors regained its affirmative stance regarding the project, and construction proceeded smoothly.

As associated architect, I had continuous friendly contact with the entire board and a cooperative working relationship with all county staff members without exception. Even Supervisor Fusselman was inclined to be friendly. He stated in public that he had nothing personal against me. When I brought change orders in for board approval, he frequently was the first to approve. He was obviously impressed with the building as it took shape, and he let me know. He was an astute politician experienced enough to realize that the voters had made a dramatically strong statement. Democracy had won. Frank Lloyd Wright indeed would have been proud!

ARCHITECTURE FOR DEMOCRACY

The previous county courthouse was situated in the center of downtown San Rafael, the county seat, as was the legality and custom of most small counties. Typical was the pseudo-Greco-Roman facade with its overscaled Doric columns and doughboy statue on the fronting lawn, bayonet ready, standing on a pedestal containing the list of community youth whose lives were lost in World War I. The doughboy figure was later moved to a location which I specifically designed as part of the landscape scheme at the north entrance to the fairgrounds to appease the small surviving group of World War I veterans. Later a statue was added to commemorate World War II veterans.

Everything relating to local government and its reflection in the pattern of business and real estate development was ripe for change. Marin County was like that of many California communities, with an influx of population following World War II and a burgeoning new economy. All aspects of the old courthouse spoke of yesterday. The nature of the governing body which met there and its main support departments all seemed antiquated. Only Vera Schultz had been a challenging voice for change. After the citizens' revolt and the advent of Peter Behr as a member of the Board of Supervisors, a refreshing new attitude became evident. Peter Behr was the shining light.* A practicing San Francisco attorney, intelligent and patient, with a charismatic sense of humor, he activated a changed demeanor within the board. In anticipation of a new environment for government, the visible skeleton of the building to come was having a subconscious effect.

After the Board of Supervisors occupied their new meeting rooms and offices, they appeared to mirror the dignity of the facility. Bickering and pettiness, a prevalent demeanor in the old courthouse, diminished. Except for occasional episodes brought on by Fusselman's historic outbursts, it could be perceived as a new body in a new environment.

The effect of Frank Lloyd Wright's "architecture for democracy" was becoming evident, just as he had predicted in his Marin speeches. The gentle curves of the roof structure took shape and the vision of a structure bridging two hills emerged. By December 1961, the 172-foot tower was hoisted into place, the signal of near completion. The Administration Building was more than eighty percent completed. The interior and exterior plastering, basic mechanical work for heating and cooling, and the rough wiring and plumbing were almost finished. Soon seventeen county departments employing 400 staff members would start moving in.

---

* Peter Behr later became a California State Senator and the legislature's leading environmentalist.

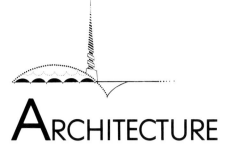

ARCHITECTURE

The overall length of the four-story Administration Building structure was 584 feet. The Hall of Justice, later added, was 880 feet long. Stairs led from one level to another with an open mall center on each level, widening as it rose, giving the effect of upward spiraling ramps. An acrylic arched skylight appeared to continue infinitely. Profuse planting enjoyed a perfect growing climate in the mall. The ensemble with exposures of glass and red and gold-anodized aluminum partition panels, separating the mall from office spaces, created a welcome, airy, immensely spacious, visual experience. This lyrical, three-dimensional composition of interior space was typical of Mr. Wright's finest works. The office ceilings were of acoustical material and flat for ease in relocating partitions, except for special architectural areas such as the library and Board of Supervisors/Planning Commission chambers. The floors were covered with custom-colored composition tile, Mr. Wright's favorite red, with terrazzo used in the entrance lobbies. The central architectural focus for the building complex was the 80-foot diameter dome with its adjoining tower as a vertical accent. The tower encased the prosaic smokestack from the heating boiler and incorporated conduit which could serve electronic or radio communication equipment for the community's future use.

Symbolically, under the central dome were located the Board of Supervisors chambers, the center of government, and the county library, the center of knowledge. Regarding the location of the library, Frank Lloyd Wright said, "It will be educational for children, to expose them to government as a point of access to the library." Nonetheless, the library had its own separate, direct entrance from the exterior of the building via a ramped walk.

The circular form of the library had a prototype from Mr. Wright's previous work, the library at Florida Southern College. One of my earliest responsibilities while a member of Mr. Wright's apprentice group, the Taliesin Fellowship, had been to develop the construction drawings for that library building. This was accomplished with Wesley Peters.

With that background experience, I finalized the layout of the Marin County Library similar to the interior layout Mr. Wright had provided for the Florida building. The control desk was located at a central point, allowing book stacks to radiate from the center around the perimeter of the circular space. The reading tables were located in the central open space. This provided maximum visual control by the library staff for all areas of the main reading room and book stack space. True to Frank Lloyd Wright's philosophy of lighting, the main read-

ing room could be lighted by glare-free, shadow-free, indirect light, with no fixtures visible. All library furnishings were custom designed to enhance basic functional aspects and were executed by the State Prison System furniture factory.

The departmental space analysis required the need for developing a flexible system of movable interior walls and partitions. Mr. Wright's concept made possible efficient and economical revisions of space needs by changing entire locations of departments or revising offices and other spaces within departments. The fact that most departmental functions of county government were of an adaptable office type made this planning technique highly effective.

As the Administration Building neared completion, most objectors disappeared or changed their minds about Frank Lloyd Wright's architecture. Everyone connected with the building seemed to enjoy it. The general contractor, Rothschild, Raffin and Weirick, was highly competent. They were proudly interested in executing the work as an asset to the community and appeared to be aware that they were creating a masterpiece of architecture. I knew from firsthand experience that the plumbers, lathers, laborers, carpenters, and sheetmetal men enjoyed the building, and their craftsmanship reflected their interest. "Mr. Wright used the same old materials," one man said to me, "it's just the way he uses them that amazes me."

"Three decades after its design, the Marin County Civic Center continues to be functionally effective, its design youthful and provocatively ahead of its time. Since many Frank Lloyd Wright buildings are approaching a century in age, his vision that the Marin Civic Center would last 300 years or more has promise of fulfillment.

After the Marin County Civic Center was completed, Frank Lloyd Wright's pendant crescents, when viewed from the interior, developed an amazing visual quality, which he must have deliberately (or intentionally) considered. Wherever we look through the arched openings, one of the many hills in the foreground or background is directly framed by that arch through which we look. Mr. Wright must now be saying, "Of course I knew that would occur."

*Views of hills framed
in architecture*

Master plan

The master plan was developed in direct relationship to the topography of the site. The prominent circular forms created abstractly by the contour lines of the surveyor's map were undoubtedly part of Mr. Wright's functional abstraction. The buildings, hills, roads, parking areas, lagoon, and prominent landscape features were joined into an ordered plan for efficient movement and interaction of people and automobiles.

In conventional planning of hilly sites, architects, planners, and developers bulldoze hills to make flat areas for automobiles and buildings, negating the natural beauty of the topography and destroying natural vegetation. Mr. Wright saw the hills as functionally, aesthetically, and structurally useful for anchoring the building to the site, the valleys between the hills for creating multiple pedestrian entrances, and the flatter areas for parking and movement of automobiles, a basic necessity for contemporary suburbia.

Mr. Wright's synthesis of the space analysis placed all major related county functions under one roof. The departments which needed functional contact were in close proximity to each other, while others, such as the sheriff's and judicial areas, were more isolated. In contrast, the county's own preliminary master plan for the site, previously developed by its planning department, had described a campus plan with a number of different buildings on a leveled site.

On occasion, I have been confronted with the criticism that the walk between some departments in the building is long. I point out that if the county's more standard master plan, calling for separate buildings had been executed, it would not only require more walking, but much of it would have to be outside, from building to building. The Frank Lloyd Wright plan has been recognized as providing remarkable savings both in time and concomitant efficiencies. Previously, the various county departments were scattered in unrelated leased spaces throughout the broad community area. This was inconvenient both for employees and citizens who had business to transact with several different departments. With administrative departments under one roof (except for justice-related facilities, which had been temporarily consolidated in the old courthouse), a new morale quickly became evident. The beauty of the transformed environment was so dramatic a change that many employees said, "I hate to go home." Others extolled the newfound advantage of having relationships close at hand with other county employees, and the ease of exchanging mutual concerns while in corridors. This was acknowledged as a wholesome new efficiency in county government.

In his projected environment for day-to-day government work, Mr. Wright pondered the existence of a jail. At first objecting, considering that it would be foreign to a beautiful circumstance, he finally agreed to the pragmatic economy and efficiency of relating the jail directly to the sheriff's facilities and courts. His ingenuity allowed the jail to be a functioning part of the complex, with separate access by the public. A humane architectural treatment placed prisoners on the top floor. The jail was successfully merged into the architecture of the whole, and although it was in a prominent location, it could not be distinguished as a jail at any exterior point from which the building could be viewed. Vehicular and pedestrian traffic to the jail was visually and physically separated from other areas of the complex.

Frank Lloyd Wright hoped that the prisoners would enjoy the benefit of the view as a rehabilitative asset. But regretfully, in my later detailed plan for the jail, I was not allowed to arrange it in that fashion because of security reasons. The cells had to be separated from exterior walls by a guarded security corridor. Had Mr. Wright lived, he would undoubtedly have evolved a way to achieve both.

FAIRGROUNDS

The master plan established the north portion of the site for a County Fair. The flat areas were adapted to various uses for exhibition, education, and recreation. Purchased by State Fair funds, this area had to be designed specifically for fair functions and needs, a one-weekend-per-year activity. But it also had to serve multipurpose needs for year-round use by a variety of citizens' groups.

The program was developed in conjunction with resourceful Marcelle McCoy Holck who was director of the Marin Art and Garden Fair, the original County Fair. That event was held annually in the city of Ross, in a much more limited area than the Civic Center site. Marcelle developed a small, but very popular, jewel-like exposition area for a beautiful annual display of ornamental horticulture plus arts and crafts, all typical of Marin County.

The desired purpose was to maintain the quality established at Ross, but to magnify the quantity and types of activities to the much larger scale of a more conventional County Fair. It had to be oriented primarily toward cultural activities rather than the typical display of farm animals and products, which were not representative of Marin County's uniqueness.

Frank Lloyd Wright's plans for the County Fair centered around a large semi-enclosed pavilion, the design of which had all the colorful, playful, festive characteristics one could imagine for a good time place. It allowed complete flexibility for the great variety of activities expected to occur under a structurally prophetic tent-like form.

Stayed suspension cables supported the tensile-textile roof stretched from tall decorative pylons, creating a festive, geometric ambience throughout the covered area of approximately three acres. At one end of the partially enclosed pavilion was an enclosed area to which the tent structure was anchored to complement its multifunctional needs.

Again Mr. Wright had designed a building ahead of its time. As part of the cost estimating process by Wesley Peters and myself, and a great deal of investigation, we determined that no satisfactory long-life fabric existed on the market to serve Mr. Wright's design properly. But Frank Lloyd Wright stated with assurance that technology would produce it. Not many years later his prediction was fulfilled, and many cable-supported tent-like structures were built around the world. In the Bay Area this type of structure has been utilized for a department store and for Bill Graham's show pavilion. Today, Dupont's Teflon fabric would serve Mr. Wright's design purpose admirably.

Unfortunately, later design and construction on the fairgrounds area were reduced in quality and were not at all in keeping with the standards established by the Frank Lloyd Wright design. The master plan relating to traffic flow and landscape screening, as well as general aesthetic standards, were seriously violated because of inadequate state and county funding plus compromises in design. At times, this portion, which includes temporary fairground facilities and an inferior exhibition building, is attributed by county officials as Frank Lloyd Wright-designed, a most grievous error.

One beautifully designed element of Frank Lloyd Wright's presentation drawings for the fairgrounds was initially in the county's program but later deleted. The amphitheatre would have seated 3,000 persons and was intended for year-round use. Its design would have accomodated musical concerts, folk dance festivals, theatre, boxing and wrestling matches, waterworks, and fireworks. Particularly emphasized were ballet aquacades and diving exhibitions.

At that time the county enjoyed a great amount of interest in a superbly trained ballet aquacade group under the direction of Gladys Hodgson. It was a particularly unique and well-attended event which later waned in popularity with the loss of its director.

After the project was under construction, a study of weather at the site determined that popular use of an amphitheatre facility would probably not succeed due to adverse climatic conditions, and it was removed from the master plan program.

It is hoped that the county government of Marin in cooperation with the California State Department of Fairs and Expositions will someday realize the importance of their opportunity to build one of Frank Lloyd Wright's most exciting plans, the Fair Pavilion. This could well replace the temporary structures now on the fairgrounds which so specifically lower the standard of the overall project in comparison with the portion which is directly related to Frank Lloyd Wright's original design and master planning.

LAGOON

The lagoon covered approximately nine acres. Frank Lloyd Wright saw it as a focal point centered amid the ensemble of buildings and roads relating directly to the pattern of the natural topography. It was also an extension of waterway which bordered the property on its northeastern corner of the bay. He envisioned that one could arrive at the Civic Center by boat as part of the good-time activities. The major part of the lagoon area was marshland, not the best for supporting structures. Since other parts of the site required fill for its development, excavation for the lagoon provided some of that requirement.

As part of the engineering analysis, I contacted a number of information sources including federal and state agencies related to water resources and development. As a result, and with a report from a consultant retained to evaluate the engineering aspects, it was determined that a considerable amount of makeup water was estimated to be required during the dry period of the year to compensate for seepage and evaporation. This could be a considerable annual expense, but at the very corner of the lagoon, where Mr. Wright's drawings indicated that a visual source of water would be developed from fountains, our excavation uncovered a natural spring which continuously seeped into the lagoon. We monitored the loss of water from the lagoon during the driest portions of the first few years, and although the water level receded somewhat, it was not nearly to the extent of the engineering estimate and did not require makeup water. In a period of serious drought during one year, the lagoon was a welcome source of added water for landscape irrigation. I often wondered to what extent Frank Lloyd Wright's intuition contributed to this.

FRANK LLOYD WRIGHT'S ADDITIONAL CONTRIBUTION

With a sense of gratitude to Mary Summers and to Marin County for the selection of Frank Lloyd Wright as architect for the Civic Center, I was later pleased to have the opportunity to assist both out of a jam. The county Planning Department, headed by Mary, had been retained by the Marin County Redevelopment Agency to develop a master plan for the northern portion of the Marin City bowl area. The Federal Housing Administration, which had jurisdiction, determined that master plan unacceptable. They claimed that the extent of grading, retaining walls, and other requirements for the steep hillside site would be too expensive to meet the objective of low-cost housing.

At that time, I was designing the Marin City Federal Housing Project* for the southern sector of the same bowl area. Mary asked me for assistance in solving the FHA problem, but there were no funds for professional consulting. Without charge, I successfully developed a new master plan for aligning the roads and for grading the site. It was also necessary to develop schematic plans for housing units to demonstrate how the new concept would be used. Instead of the flat lots, which would have been created by the rejected plan, my plan elevated the houses on piers, to "float" over the terrain. The designs illustrated use for either a downhill or an uphill approach from roads carefully tailored to the contours of the site to minimize grading.

The FHA accepted our concept and plans, and the project went ahead.

---

*The Marin City Project was a joint venture of Aaron G. Green, F.A.I.A. and John C. Warnecke, F.A.I.A. Aaron Green was the architect for design.

"Pole houses," later designed by architect Vernon De Mars for the successful bidding developer, were based on our schematic planning which was made mandatory by the Redevelopment Agency.

In 1964 the Marin City Federal Housing Project was awarded the First Honor Award by the Federal Housing and Home Financing Agency in competition with over 700 other such projects throughout the country. It was designated by housing officials as the breakthrough project to new federal housing standards. This project was an early recognition of the Civil Rights Movement and another social milestone in Marin County for a higher standard of architecture: "architecture for democracy" via Frank Lloyd Wright.

Without my training by Frank Lloyd Wright for organic relationships of buildings to sites, I could not have developed these accomplishments. *Therefore, the Marin City Federal Housing Project may be considered another contribution to Marin County by Frank Lloyd Wright.*

Frank Lloyd Wright and apprentice Aaron Green at Taliesin, 1940.

CONSTRUCTION PROCESS

Considering the unique design and advanced building techniques, the entire construction process of the Administration Building went remarkably smoothly. Many factors contributed to its success. The structural relationship of elements inherent in Frank Lloyd Wright's concept created an admirable simplicity of construction technique.

The Taliesin Associated Architects, headed by Wesley Peters, did a superb job of developing the construction documents relating structural aspects and basic architectural details. Their effort was coordinated with interior layouts, site development work, cabinetwork, furnishings, and general specifications, all of which were developed in my San Francisco office. This cooperative handling of the day-to-day problems continued by mail, telephone, and telex.

Particularly important to the success of the project was the astute help I received from David Tirrell, A.I.A., my assistant project architect. David efficiently kept track of the myriad of detailed construction items and conditions in a clear and concise form and could always smooth out ruffled feelings with

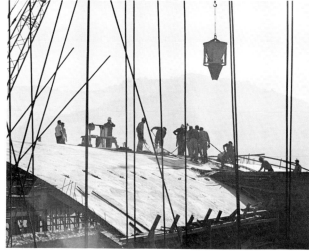

Construction

his unflappable and friendly demeanor. David served through most of the construction period of the Administration Building and throughout construction of the Hall of Justice and the Auditorium.

Another positive factor was the close relationship maintained with full-time project inspector, Clement Finney, regarding all details of work. Clem had been recommended for the position by me but was employed by the county. He had done an exemplary job in similar construction of the Marin City Federal Housing project. The architects depended much on Clem's alertness and technical judgment.

Also significant was the experience and skill of the general contractor's job-superintendent, Emil Storm, a tough, seasoned expert of the old school. Emil, who was the master of any construction problem, made the most difficult problems seem easy. He developed a simple forming system for construction of the thin-shell concrete barrel-arched roof and the thin-shell dome of the library.

The success of the overall project was assisted by the active cooperation of the general contractor, Rothschild, Raffin and Weirick. This firm was imbued with a sense of the project's importance and its relationship to the community, treating the opportunity as a privilege. A very close handling of the job thereby developed between the major partners in the construction activity.

The county staff was kept involved in the daily construction status, particularly the Department of Public Works and its affiliated Building Inspection Department. Public Works Director Donald Frost, who had succeeded Marvin Brigham, was an excellent structural and civil engineer and a knowledgeable consultant. He and his assistant, Art Knutson, were always involved when consideration of structural circumstances and alternatives developed.

Six years later, construction of the Hall of Justice was not quite as smooth and was beset by many daily problems. Although experienced and generally efficient, the contracting firm's attitude with the Hall of Justice hinged upon being an out-of-state firm. The job's smaller scope apparently was not as important as its larger business interests. The main concern seemed to be profit. The architects, who quickly surmised this, notified the county's staff, including the Public Works Director and the county counsel, Douglas Maloney, to carefully document all aspects of the work in a defensive, legal manner. From the beginning, it seemed to me that the contractor expected to develop a paper train of documentation toward a suit for damages claiming delay. In the end, we learned that our suspicions were correct. The architects' defensive documentation with the county staff during the process was beneficial.

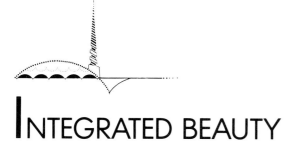

INTEGRATED BEAUTY

The original aesthetic concept developed by Mr. Wright was remarkably complete, functionally and technically. The achievement negated the rumor that Frank Lloyd Wright designs were always expensive. The Marin County Civic Center was built at a cost no more than most ordinary buildings for that purpose and was less costly than many. The advanced technology using precast concrete and prestressed concrete elements, proved to be a straightforward construction technique, combining concrete and steel in a most economical manner as Mr. Wright had originally stated.

The basic construction of the building was a synthesis of state-of-the-art building techniques combined with uses of well-known materials. Compared to contemporary standard buildings, it was an articulated, relatively lightweight, flexible structure. Typical of Mr. Wright's organic architecture philosophy, the structure was in-and-of the hills, integrated sensitively to the topography rather than being placed on the site.

The assemblage of floors utilized a system of precast, prestressed double-tee floor members manufactured at the nearby Petaluma plant of Ben C. Gerwick Company. Vertical supports were primarily small-diameter extra-strength steel columns with a precast concrete cover, elliptical shaped. The roof system was composed of a series of precast concrete trusses supporting a thin-shell, barrel-arch of reinforced concrete. Calculations for the precast concrete elements were made by the San Francisco firm of T. Y. Lin, a preeminent authority in the design of prestressed, precast concrete. The multiplicity of similar precast elements, and the speed with which the basic system could be erected, contributed to the unusual economy of construction.

Contrary to popular opinion, there were virtually no luxury materials in the building, with the exception of minor quantities of gold-anodized aluminum for decorative accents. So small a quantity was employed in proportion to the entire structure that its cost was almost negligible. The gold-anodized aluminum accent was like a string of pearls on a basic black dress.

An important design concept was the decorated concrete barrel-arch roof construction. Placing precast ornamental units on the roof over the barrel shell overcame any appearances of imprecise workmanship, which otherwise would have been evident. This meant that the roof shell did not have to be an exact labor-intensive effort because the ornament itself visually overrode it. Similarly, the decorative facias (roof edges), the spheres, made it possible for the long, extended, straight-line roof edges to be visually tolerable as they disguised variations in line. These simple decorative construction devices achieved economy in addition to giving the assemblage an intrinsic, integrated beauty, which Frank Lloyd Wright referred to as organic decoration.

Seismic Design

The seismic design of the Marin Civic Center has become highly controversial, an interesting throwback to the illusions which hovered around Frank Lloyd Wright's past. During most of Mr. Wright's career, beginning from his earliest practice, the claim was often made by conservative engineering minds that his structures were not in accord with current engineering standards. It is now known worldwide that his principles and concepts were ahead of their time, intuitively correct structurally and invariably confirmed on those occasions when actual load tests were carried out. Moreover, the application of standard building code formulae were frequently not relevant since they had not been developed in anticipation of his nonstandard, innovative conditions. For instance, his design of the Johnson Wax Administration Building columns was not accepted by Wisconsin State engineers whose calculations indicated they would fail. After an actual load test proved that a column would carry six times its design load before any possibility of failure, it was allowed to be built. Similarly, his design for the famous Kaufmann house, "Fallingwater," was claimed inadequate. After fifty years, it is in good condition and visited each year by many thousands of tourists. Mr. Wright's Imperial Hotel, with its unique foundation system, was the only major building in Tokyo to resist the 8.3 magnitude earthquake of 1923.*

In the Marin project, Frank Lloyd Wright foresaw the long slender buildings being subjected to the undulations of seismic movements as they spanned from one hill to another. Thus, he conceived the building structurally as sections, with expansion joints from the roof all the way through to the foundation. This would allow for articulation of the sections if and when undulating movements of the ground occurred. It was this conceptual circumstance which guided his structural engineer, Mendel Glickman, to carry through in the design. Glickman had provided structural engineering calculations for many of Mr. Wright's most

---

*See appendix for comments by Louis Sullivan on seismic design of the Imperial Hotel.

famous buildings and was in tune with Mr. Wright's innovative engineering concepts. He was a deeply respected professional who for many years directed the Structural Engineering Department at the University of Oklahoma. The county submitted engineering calculations for review to the International Conference of Building Officials in Los Angeles. This was the official agency in charge of developing and interpreting the building code. The engineers of this legal entity insisted that the foundations of the building be tied together, not allowing the expansion joints to continue down through the foundations. This reduced the effectiveness of Frank Lloyd Wright's engineering concept to some extent.

The structural engineering calculations for the Hall of Justice were developed with the help of a local Bay Area licensed structural engineer engaged as Glickman's assistant. There were many meetings with the engineers of the International Conference of Building Officials. After intensive, detailed considerations and various modifications of the structural design, the building permit was obtained.

The Civic Center buildings survived the October 1989 earthquake of 7.1 magnitude with no damage, disproving the disparaging engineers who want to waste millions of taxpayers' dollars to make it "earthquake proof."

FRANK LLOYD WRIGHT ON BUILDING CODES

Excerpted from an address in 1939, Frank Lloyd Wright is quoted here regarding building codes:

> "The building codes embody, of course, only what the previous generation knew or thought about building, and the ensuing generation finds the code a stumbling block. When I was called to build the building in Tokyo, I could not get a permit to build it. Nor could I get a building permit or full permission to build the S. C. Johnson Wax building either. It is sometimes necessary to say: After all, buildings are for life and life goes on. If you want to confine all that the next generation or this generation is going to know about building to what the past generation knew, go ahead and stop our building

(i.e., restrict new and better ideas). The illiberal administration of these building codes is due directly to the antiquated educational processes that have produced the men who make the codes.

"The desire to hold to rules and regulations that prevent progress is not characteristic of a democracy, but, of course, committee work is slow work at best, and democracy is a kind of committee at work."

SKYLIGHTS

Frank Lloyd Wright wanted the building's interior central mall open to the sky. Natural air-conditioning, he called it. After his death, it was deemed necessary to cover the mall with a skylight. Wesley Peters designed the barrel-arch vaulted skylight, repeating the adjoining roof forms and carrying out the continuous linear space concept created by Mr. Wright. This was one of the most striking visual features of the building's interior. Since no such skylight had previously been built, we worked closely with a well-known skylight manufacturer and the Rohm and Haas Company, manufacturers of clear acrylic (Plexiglas) sheet to develop the fabrication and installation details. The length of the Plexiglas sheet required to span the full width of the skylighted area was 20 feet, but the material was not manufactured in that length, thereby necessitating two joints in each bay. We developed a detail which butted the two ends of the Plexiglas sheets together and joined them with a bead of expandable silicon, which from previous experience, we considered a highly effective material. Rohm and Haas engineers disagreed with the design and insisted that a rigidly glued plastic coverplate over the joint would be necessary.

The skylight was installed with the joint they designed, and it proved inadequate to handle movement caused by thermal expansion and contraction of the materials. Therefore it leaked. This was embarrassing at the official opening dedication day when serious rain occurred.

Of course, the cliché was automatically heard that Frank Lloyd Wright's buildings always leaked. And, of course, Mr. Wright was in no way responsible for this deficiency. Most architects have some problems with leaking roofs caused by inadequacy of workmanship or materials, but they rarely attract the same publicity as Frank Lloyd Wright.

Later, in building the Hall of Justice, similar skylights were constructed, using a single piece of clear acrylic. In the interim, a manufacturing process had been developed which extruded 20-foot lengths of the material and produced a satisfactory nonleaking condition. The county later decided to remove the original jointed units in the Administration Building and replace them with the full-length acrylic sections. Unfortunately, they did not engage the architect's assistance and allowed a faulty installation with insufficient engagement on each side of the installed sheet to allow for thermal movement, thereby developing a different type of leaking problem. Blame is still cast upon Frank Lloyd Wright when buckets are evident in rainy weather.

The skylight design has become so popular that it is now a standard skylight form available from the catalogs of most skylight manufacturers. The proliferation of this design has spread throughout the country into many building types, including shopping malls, schools, office buildings, and others. The design origin, of course, is uncredited.

BIG PINK AND THE BLUE ROOF COLOR

Frank Lloyd Wright wanted a golden roof color to match the gold of the hills. His drawings, as well as the scale model built for the county, incorporated the gold roof and indicated the color of walls for the buildings.

Interestingly coincidental and despite the passage of time, we experienced the same technical difficulty which, legend has it, prevented the Golden Gate Bridge from having a gold finish instead of its prime coat red. At that time, no paint or coating had been developed which would maintain a gold color when exposed to exterior conditions without rather quickly tarnishing to a dull and unpleasant dirty brown. After much investigation, such as involving automotive paint manufacturers in research, we reluctantly had to look for an alternate solution.

At Taliesin Mrs. Frank Lloyd Wright had assumed the responsibility of color selection after her husband's death. This was a continuation of her role in assisting him in similar decisions. Considering what Frank Lloyd Wright would have selected, she and her staff decided to exercise his choice for the closest design-related building he had recently developed. The Greek Orthodox Church near Milwaukee, Wisconsin, which had a domed roof similar in size to that of the Marin project, was under construction concurrently. Mr. Wright had decided the roof of that dome would have a blue mosaic tile covering to relate to the sky blue background. The conclusion was to use a similar blue color for the Marin project roof and the sand beige color for the walls, which Frank Lloyd Wright had used on the original scale model.

Since we well knew the fading characteristics of the sun's ultraviolet rays plus oxidation affected by weathering in general, we decided to install the originally selected colors with more intensive hues in order to allow for the anticipated fading. As usual, Frank Lloyd Wright projects provided a new, nonstandard appearance, often color-related. While many people applauded the positive use of colors, those more conservative questioned the selection. Often the question has been asked, "How did the blue color selection for the roof come about?" At times the local media referred to the project as "Big Pink," perhaps more lovingly than derisively.

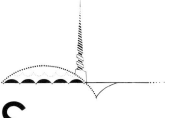

SAN QUENTIN FURNITURE FACTORY

I began looking into the possibility of separate contracts for construction of the cabinetwork and custom furnishings. The California Prison System provided tax-supported municipalities within the state the opportunity to purchase their prison-built office furniture. Because of labor union considerations, it was against the law for prison officials to cut costs below market value in competition with private industry.

Glenn Thorpe, sales manager for the California Correctional Industries, was eager to discuss the possibilities of providing all the furniture and cabinetwork. Although their standard furniture was ordinary and ungainly, I realized the manufacturing quality was excellent. Mr. Thorpe agreed with my offer to redesign some of the furniture and asked me to submit sketches and suggestions. I redesigned some pieces but maintained their original construction. One model became the basic chair used in the Civic Center and was one of the major purchases from the prison factory.

Mr. Thorpe was apprehensive about executing custom designs. The prison factory's manufacturing experience had been related only to their mass-produced catalog furniture, but nevertheless Mr. Thorpe decided to cooperate with our plan.

During the year that followed, the inmates at the San Quentin furniture factory provided the custom-designed furniture and cabinetwork as well as the standard office furniture catalog ordered for the project. The walnut furniture was consistent with the woodwork throughout the structure. The prison industry organizations were competent, easy to work with, and met their time schedules.

Their success with the Administration Building work meant that they would later be authorized also to provide the custom millwork and furniture for the Hall of Justice. That later order was much larger and more complex. They constructed the custom millwork and furniture for the courtrooms as well as many furniture items for the jail. The process was very interesting. I was required to make many trips to San Quentin, where I was officially escorted through the prison yards to the furniture factory. I was frequently in contact with inmates who were working on the drawings. Years later, I occasionally received letters from these inmates asking if they could work for me upon their release. No one ever showed up in person. San Quentin was for felons who had little probability of release.

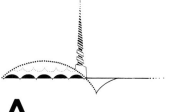

ADMINISTRATION BUILDING DEDICATION

Finally on October 13, 1962, the dedication ceremony was held. More than 400 people braved fog and rain for the flag raising. The only concession to the weather was to have the speeches delivered inside. Mrs. Wright told the assembled visitors, "My husband believed that heaven was on this earth and that this earth was divine and should be beautified. He never put anything on paper until he had conceived the whole project in his head. And this, I think, is the true spirit of the artist." She then recalled the first time Mr. Wright had inspected the site for the Civic Center. He returned home and exclaimed, "What a site! What a site! Wait till you see what I'm going to do with that site."

The principal speaker at the dedication was Dr. Theodore A. Gill, president of the San Francisco Theological Seminary. He said, "The citizens of Marin were reluctant to pour money into one vast ho-hum, so they took a chance on art. Suddenly we see what one superb dreamer saw. The building is vigorously idiosyncratic like its creator, but it has grace and dignity and power."

After the morning ceremonies, visitors spent the day touring. By noontime, the rain had become torrential, yet more and more people arrived. It was sad that Frank Lloyd Wright was not present to witness this. He had died ten months before ground was broken, but his hand had been in control almost until the final completion of the drawings.

The Administration Building had cost $22.87 per square foot, about $1.00 per square foot less than the county's last major construction, the Courthouse Annex in San Rafael, a prosaic stereotyped building erected in 1959.

HALL OF JUSTICE

It was my responsibility to define future needs and develop a final space analysis for the Hall of Justice. I collected detailed information on the site conditions, soil and weather, as well as road and highway traffic, zoning changes, and all needs of the county departments.

The Marin County Hall of Justice became a turning point in the design of courts throughout the United States, and a new interest in that subject catalyzed from this design project. Oregon's Judge William Fort and I sponsored a joint national committee linking the American Bar Association and the American Institute of Architects to promote more perceptive courtroom design. A Ford Foundation grant awarded to the committee resulted in an in-depth study titled *The American Courthouse.* Published under the committee's auspices, this book later provided a much-needed professional reference. In judicial circles, the Marin Court facilities quickly became well known, and the designs of many courtrooms across the country have been strongly affected by the Marin prototype. Among early ones were thirteen courtrooms in the Municipal Court Building of Washington, D. C., and the experimental Courtroom of the Future at McGeorge Law School, College of the Pacific in Sacramento, California, for which I was design consultant. Also there were many requests for courts design information or assistance nationally, and some internationally.*

Following are some excerpts from "Trials of an Architect" which I wrote for the *Journal of the American Judicature Society,* just prior to construction of the Hall of Justice:

> "Since few architects have the opportunity to design more than one, or even one court facility in a lifetime, programming demanded conscientious in-depth analysis. I contacted the Marin County presiding judges with hopes of discussion meetings, but since they had recently cooperated with another architect in developing a program for a temporary annex, and they were not in favor of the new decentralized location, I was denied meetings with the judiciary.

> "Administrative analysis established the number of courts to be programmed for this site as adequate to population growth for the next twenty-five years, with branch courts for more remote concentrations of population beyond that time. The architects were authorized to prepare the drawings for construction of the Hall of Justice which had been designed by Frank Lloyd Wright in preliminary form to attach to the already completed Administration Building of Mr. Wright's design.

> "I was determined to proceed with research in court procedures and to make of this court building a functional concept, doing justice to Mr. Wright's magnificent overall architectural concept. Marin County judges finally became interested, and to some extent even enthusiastic, about the process of designing a new type of court facility as I proposed.

---

* See letters from Supreme Courts of Hawaii and Tasmania on Page 129.

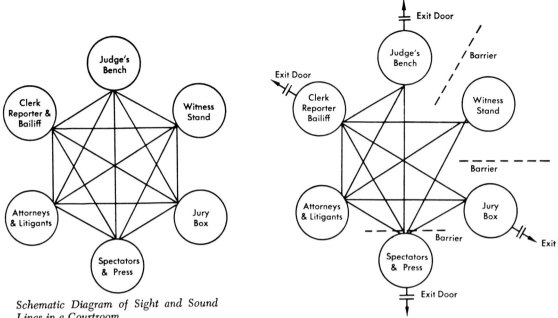

Schematic Diagram of Sight and Sound Lines in a Courtroom.

Schematic Diagram of Direct Walking Access Lines in a Courtroom.

Schematic Diagram of Courtroom-Related Functions.

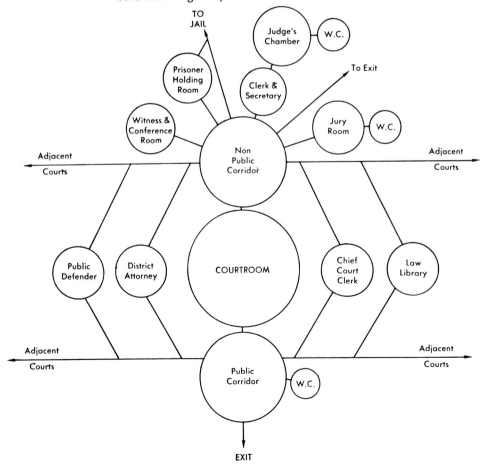

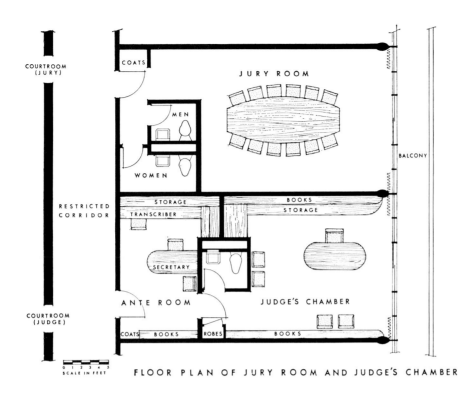

COURTROOM (JURY)

RESTRICTED CORRIDOR

COURTROOM (JUDGE)

COATS

JURY ROOM

BALCONY

MEN

WOMEN

STORAGE
TRANSCRIBER

BOOKS
STORAGE

SECRETARY

ANTE ROOM

JUDGE'S CHAMBER

COATS | BOOKS | ROBES | BOOKS

0 1 2 3 4 5
SCALE IN FEET

FLOOR PLAN OF JURY ROOM AND JUDGE'S CHAMBER

COURTROOM PLANS

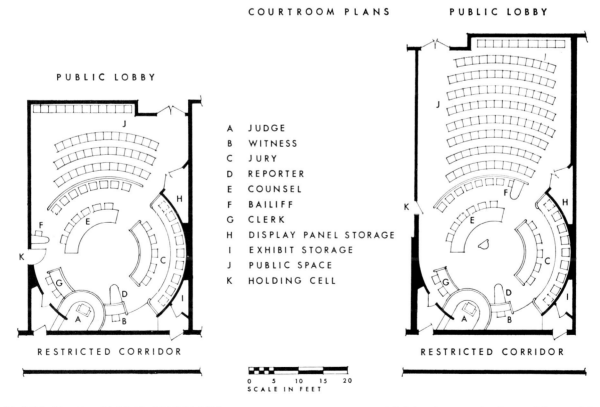

PUBLIC LOBBY

PUBLIC LOBBY

A JUDGE
B WITNESS
C JURY
D REPORTER
E COUNSEL
F BAILIFF
G CLERK
H DISPLAY PANEL STORAGE
I EXHIBIT STORAGE
J PUBLIC SPACE
K HOLDING CELL

RESTRICTED CORRIDOR

RESTRICTED CORRIDOR

0 5 10 15 20
SCALE IN FEET

FLOOR PLAN – 50 SEAT COURTROOM

FLOOR PLAN – 100 SEAT COURTROOM

"A search for published information on the design of courts eventually covered dozens of legal and governmental organizations and revealed that even a normal amount of reference material did not exist. Apparently, the apathy regarding the design of better courthouses was not only local, but national as well. It became dismally obvious that there had been no new thinking in court design for the past 150 years, and that tradition still dominated logic in many important buildings, both municipal and federal.

"We analyzed plans of twenty-five courts newly constructed or in design stage from all areas of California. Our conclusion: Not only did none of them incorporate new functional ideas, but in many cases basic functional violations were being permanently constructed into these buildings.

"As our research continued, we acquired the support of the Marin County Bar Association, as well as the Municipal and Superior Court Judges. The Administration Building had by now become a widely acclaimed functional and artistic success. Since it had been constructed without premium costs, even conservative-minded taxpayers admitted its success, which was dramatically confirmed when the citizens voted a bond issue of over $7 million to fund construction of the Hall of Justice, the first county bond issue successfully passed in twenty-five years.

"As a strong, collaborative effort with the associated architects of the Frank Lloyd Wright Foundation, we had developed an overall relationship within the building, which related court and law enforcement facilities with other governmental activities. It was an ideal culmination.

"Frank Lloyd Wright did not live to see the construction of the only building he designed for governmental use. Construction of the first phase of the Administration Building was carried out by Mr. Wright's staff and myself and has been profoundly successful, both functionally and artistically. It has truly performed as Frank Lloyd Wright predicted at the time of his presenting the designs: 'Here is a crucial opportunity to open the eyes, not of Marin County alone, but of the entire country, to what officials gathering together might themselves do to broaden and beautify human lives'."

JAIL

In 1963 the administrative and space analyses which I authored for the Hall of Justice contained the basis for the design I executed for the now-existing jail. The decision was to develop a holding facility with a capacity for 100 prisoners. The Marin County sheriff predicted that this number would accommodate the average requirement for many years, after which time the previously programmed Honor Farm would be scheduled for construction. At that time, a contractual arrangement existed with Sonoma County which had excess jail space to accommodate some of Marin's prisoners at peak periods.

The State Board of Corrections had estimated in 1960 that a complete jail facility would require accommodations for 197 prisoners. Development of an honor camp was targeted for 1970 or earlier. The report indicated that the sheriff's lower prediction was based on historical statistics of a Marin County inmate population considerably less in comparison to population of most counties. It was also assumed that the nature of Marin County's population would remain principally residential, of high economic level, and with little change in increase of prisoner population.

Today this once-relaxed bedroom community, primarily serving professional and white-collar commuters to San Francisco, has developed a regrettably large attraction for drug dealers and users, which has exacerbated crime statistics and estimates of jail inmate population.

As a result, governing officials are succumbing to pressures to build a monstrously oversized jail facility of completely negative and insensitive architectural proportions. The proposed facility is to be located prominently on the Civic Center site, but inefficiently detached from the courts and ancillary justice facilities. This is destined to do irreparable harm to the character of this important complex and will provide a reprehensible ambience focusing on criminal incarceration rather than the original direction of Frank Lloyd Wright.

Constructing a very large jail facility estimated at many millions of dollars for construction alone would incur tremendous added costs to Marin citizens. But the cost of construction is only the "tip of the iceberg" of total costs. The attendant costs for guarding and handling the prisoners, costs for facilities, and salaries of the related judicial staff (including judges, courts, and sheriff's personnel) must be seriously increased to relate to the processing, arraignment, trial, sentencing, and housing of such a prisoner population. That emerges to gigantic proportions as a permanent annual cost, and far exceeds the initial one-time construction cost of the jail building.

It would be better in all respects if law enforcement, treatment, and education were to be funded at a percentage of those costs to extricate the county from its exaggerated drug-related crime conditions. Creative law enforcement together with enlightened criminal justice application could serve the immediate needs of the community rather than the excessive construction of hotel facilities for criminals. For those who seek a more relaxed environment within a cultural suburban setting, their environment is being threatened. Let us hope that the spirit of previous governing officials, once so courageous and forward in their thinking as to develop the Frank Lloyd Wright Civic Center, can inspire similar high standards toward a better solution of this serious threat within their community.

Social Furor

On August 7, 1970, the Marin County Civic Center became an object of national focus. A trial from nearby San Quentin Prison was being held in one of the county courtrooms and exploded into violence. A tragic scene occurred when Judge Harold Haley, much loved by the community, was taken hostage by the prisoners and shot during their attempt to escape. The prisoner on trial, George Jackson, was shot and killed with two other prisoners, James D. McClain and William A. Christmas. District Attorney Gary Thomas was shot and as a result paralyzed. He later became one of Marin County's judges.

The incarceration and trial of Angela Davis, accused of assisting that escape operation, intensified national interest in the case. As part of the upheaval, one of the courtrooms was bombed and destroyed and had to be rebuilt.

The officials in charge became obsessed with security. Fortunately, they were sensitive to the importance of the building's design and desired to secure it with as little aesthetic alteration as possible. The architects were called in to meet this challenge. All technological considerations were reviewed. Various electronic systems were installed in combination with such restraints as barred areas and added doors. Courtrooms were revised to install bulletproof shields to protect judges. Panic button systems were initiated, and one courtroom was developed as a super-security facility for especially sensitive trials.

The building was adapted to this serious functional change with minimum damage. The security barred areas were designed in a decorative manner, complementing the building's established aesthetic character. Most electronic devices had minimum visibility.

After the searing violence, I designed a memorial area adjoining the Hall of Justice to honor Judge Harold Haley. The memorial includes a grove of living trees and circular platforms, with a large natural rock containing an incised statement commemorating the judge. A permanent concrete bench invites one to pause in reflection.

Veterans Memorial Auditorium

After Mr. Wright's death, the planning process for the Marin County Fair resulted in pressures from the veterans, who had been politically promised a veterans memorial building. A plan was developed to expedite a multipurpose building on the fairgrounds portion of the overall site. It was decided, after much deliberation with State Fair authorities, that the building could be one of the state-financed facilities if it met criteria for fair uses. Together with joint funds contributed by the county from the Veterans Memorial Building Fund, the project became the Veterans Memorial Auditorium, later named the Marin Center Auditorium.

Located on the fairground site, the building utilized adjacent parking areas. This was a reasonable revision of the original Frank Lloyd Wright master plan which had followed the county's program of locating an auditorium on the county-owned portion of the site. This modification also freed additional parking area for the Administration Building and Hall of Justice.

The auditorium's program of use became a political issue. The veterans group politicized for a flat-floor facility to hold various activities including military drills. The County Fair program was varied and could use either flat-floor space or fixed auditorium seating space with stage facilities, or both. Many active groups had developed around more culturally oriented activities, such as the symphony, the ballet, and theatre. Community leaders believed that the cultural activities were growing fast and would continue to be the most seriously needed. The issue was stalemated because of the commitment made over the years that the county was putting aside funds to develop the veterans building.

To overcome the impasse, I volunteered to develop a complete survey and analysis of the county's needs by contacting groups serving cultural and non-cultural activities. Meetings were held, and a questionnaire distributed throughout the county requested information as to potential use, frequency of use, numbers of persons involved, etc. The tabulated results indicated conclusively that the main interest in the community was directed toward a culturally oriented facility.

A combined use program developed which required a near-impossible solution: a combination or convertible multiple-use building which could accommodate both flat-floor and tiered seating of conventional auditorium design for symphony, ballet, and traveling or local theatre. The budget was very restricted and the task appeared insurmountable. To satisfy the variety of program uses normally would require two buildings of different characteristics.

The building design presented to the county was the product of Taliesin Senior Architect Wesley Peters with the illustrious George Izenour of Yale University as technical theatre design consultant. I was the associated architect.

The solution was extremely innovative in many technical and functional respects. The flat-floor area was separated from the conventional tiered seating area by using an 80-foot-long movable wall. By moving this huge wall, the volume in the theatre could be reduced, making it more acoustically ideal for theatre productions, small musical concerts, and smaller audiences. For large events requiring greater interior volume, such as symphony, opera, or band concerts, the movable acoustic wall could be retracted, allowing a greater volume and more seating. When a larger amount of flat-floor space was required for exhibits, expositions, or veterans' use, the movable wall was repositioned. To arrive at this unique solution, a completely new type of tiered folding seating had to be developed.

A first design would have functionally served as a full theatre or auditorium with adequate dressing room facilities, storage facilities, and rehearsal hall facilities. This proposal was too large for the county's limited budget appropriation, and the supervisors requested that it be reduced. The second version, which was constructed within the approved budget, unfortunately required eliminating many spaces which should have been included. Some desirable multipurpose uses of the facility have been restricted as a result of the omissions.

Nonetheless, the auditorium has been fully used and has demonstrated the validity of the analysis indicating the county's need for a culturally oriented facility. The Marin Symphony and Opera have thrived, and a continuous schedule of traveling shows, lectures, and concerts have filled the hall. Unlike many elaborate and expensive performing arts buildings in the country which have been notable acoustical failures, this modest, low-cost facility has been acclaimed for its fine acoustics by San Francisco music critics and well-known performers alike.

Maintaining Quality

A major problem for architects is to maintain the quality of their designed projects after construction is complete and the building is entirely under the care of its owner. Particularly in Frank Lloyd Wright's buildings, the harmony and effectiveness of the entire opus is most sensitive to the relationships of all its parts. Every small part is a considered portion of the design and contributes to its unique quality.

When an untrained person, however well intentioned, makes modifications of color, furniture, textiles, landscaping, or of major considerations as remodeling, without consulting the architect or without sensitive comprehension of what is required to retain the original harmony, the project is bound to suffer major harm. The threat is continuous, particularly in a governmental building where those in charge, elected or appointed, have limited tenure, and those newly in office tend to change things (the new broom sweeps clean syndrome).

For nearly three decades after construction of the Marin project, many persons in temporary charge of county government departments such as Planning, Parks and Recreation, Public Works, Landscape Design, as well as department heads who relate purely to the functional use of space, have exercised assumed prerogatives to modify some aspects of the Civic Center complex.

It is amazing that despite such circumstances, the quality of the project is so well preserved today. This is testament both to the strength of its overall design and the successful resistance of some officials in government (whose tenure has been more continuous). They have been able to sensitively circumvent some harmful changes, but not all.

Nonetheless there are continuous pressures, well intentioned but insensitive, to introduce unfortunate changes which could be constructively directed if good ground rules plus a system of monitoring them were developed. It would be in the interest of the Marin County citizens if this were accomplished to preserve their unique and extremely valuable treasure.

As a result of the increasing need, a movement is simmering within the county which can help handle this dilemma. An ad hoc committee has developed, comprised of several people personally interested in preserving the quality of the project: Joan Brown, coordinator for Civic Center volunteers; Dick Shaler, architect and longtime employee of the Public Works Department who worked with the project architects during the construction period; Sally Hauser, lead docent; and Jerry Houston, an archivist who has organized county files, particularly in reference to the Frank Lloyd Wright Civic Center project. They are petitioning county officials to create an objective commission to oversee all issues and conditions related to modifications and visual aspects of the Civic Center. Hope exists that such a commission may be delegated.

The makeup of such a commission will determine its effectiveness. It would seem most effective if this type of commission were given a detailed set of specifications and guidelines as an overall frame of reference for decisions regarding changes. It is hoped that the current Board of Supervisors will recognize the importance of their responsibility as conservators of this uniquely active, historical treasure, and that they will do everything possible to preserve the Civic Center's integrity and value for present and future citizens.

In 1972 after fifteen years of intense, dedicated effort, I resigned my association with the project. This was a result of growing dissatisfaction and frustration, stemming from the deteriorating standard of the new work beyond the auditorium site area, plus the lessening of county officials' support for a better standard. I also felt it was time to concentrate on my own professional work. However, with serious concern for the county's stake in the project and concern for continued friendship with the Taliesin group, I assisted in making a smooth administrative transition by providing Architect William Schwarz from my office as my replacement.

Bill was a mature and competent architect familiar with the Marin project in detail. Originally my student at Stanford University, he proceeded to Taliesin as an apprentice for several years after Mr. Wright's death and then joined my staff. Bill continues his efforts as liaison between the Frank Lloyd Wright Foundation and the county. With some frustration, he continually attempts to elevate understanding and the standard of execution of the work.

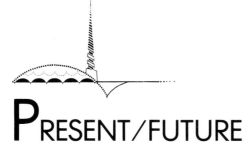

PRESENT/FUTURE

In my Marin County Government Space Analysis for the Hall of Justice, dated November 4, 1963, the following statement was included, which now seems a proper current summation:

"The architects take this opportunity to reemphasize the significance and potential value to Marin County of a great architectural concept, one of the last and most important works of Frank Lloyd Wright. Here, as an important episode in the history of our Republic, officials and workers, and, in fact, all the citizens of the county and its many visitors may enjoy the beneficent effects of a beautiful planned environment for work, governance, and cultural activities.

"Here, the intangible force of a noble architectural concept, humanizing the accomplishments of the machine and of purely objective science, can constantly provide inspiration for the intellect, emotions, and heart: the opportunity to live and work in a beautiful integrated space relaxing the eyes and mind by absorbing distant natural views framed by the graceful geometry of the foreground architecture.

"Here, the latent power of a great artist's genius can exert its force for the future, enriching the hours and lives of the governmental employees of Marin County as well as of those thousands of owners, users, and participants.

"Such a building and environment provide for younger generations a rare opportunity as they use the facilities of library, fairgrounds, parks and playgrounds devoted to their interests. Children exposed to such an environment may well retain in future years the connotation of dignity and beauty associated with civic enterprise and government. The total effect is invaluable. This is indeed architecture for democracy.

"This heritage from Frank Lloyd Wright is a magnificent, invaluable treasure. Marin County's Board of Supervisors deserves the gratitude and appreciation of present and future generations for wisely securing the benefits of this architectural ideal."

Wesley Peters, Aaron Green, Mary Summers, and Vera Schultz
on occasion of the 25th anniversary of the Administration Building,
October 13, 1987.

"*The* community center would mean more because it would be a salient feature of every countryside development of the county, wherever the county seat might be. The civic center would always be an attractive automobile objective — perhaps situated just off some major highway in interesting landscape — noble and inspiring."

"*No* free man in modern America needs to box or hole-in for protection any more in any building or needs to dive into his burrow in any city. Danger is there. Security in every sense is best found in the new free spacing and integral construction of scientific decentralization."

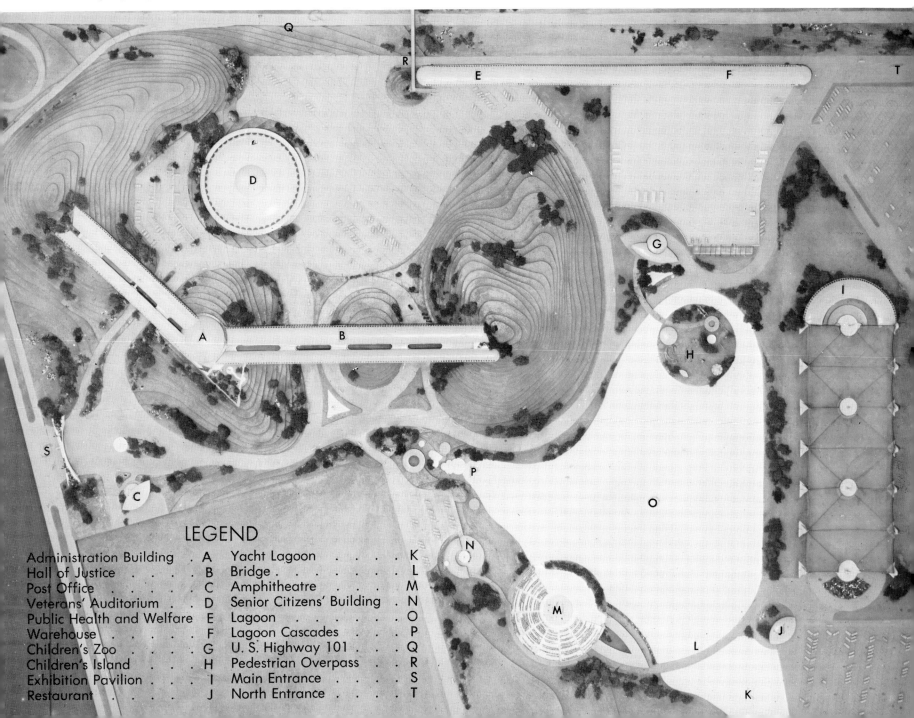

Photograph of original project model

LEGEND

Administration Building	A	Yacht Lagoon	K
Hall of Justice	B	Bridge	L
Post Office	C	Amphitheatre	M
Veterans' Auditorium	D	Senior Citizens' Building	N
Public Health and Welfare	E	Lagoon	O
Warehouse	F	Lagoon Cascades	P
Children's Zoo	G	U. S. Highway 101	Q
Children's Island	H	Pedestrian Overpass	R
Exhibition Pavilion	I	Main Entrance	S
Restaurant	J	North Entrance	T

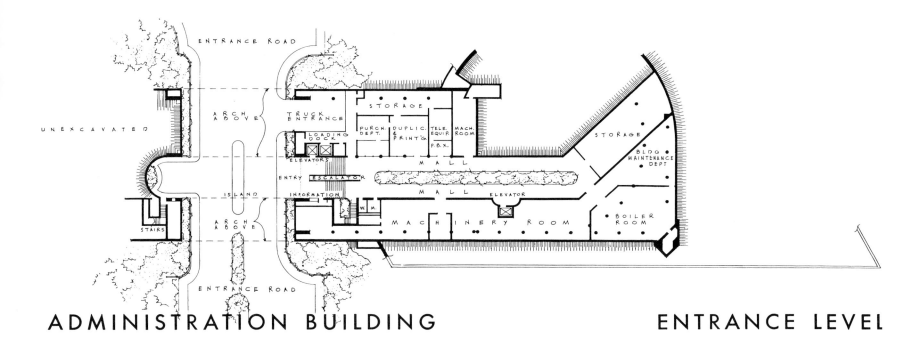

ADMINISTRATION BUILDING

ENTRANCE LEVEL

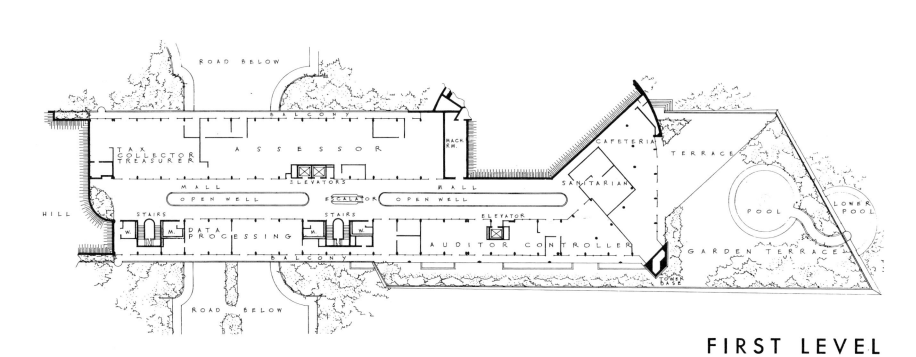

FIRST LEVEL

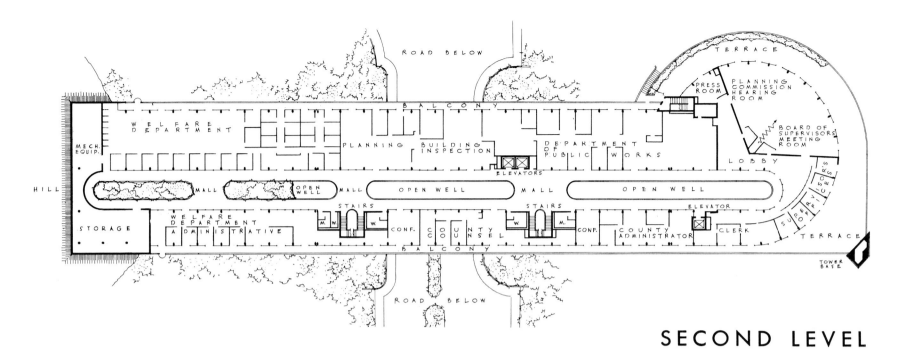

SECOND LEVEL

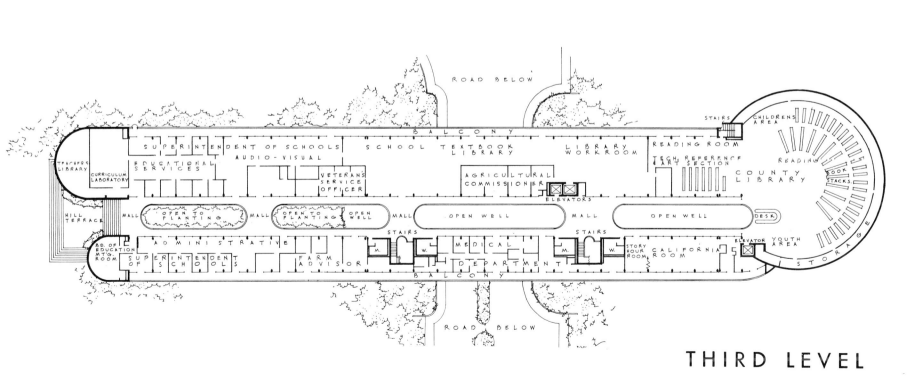

THIRD LEVEL

"*With a sense of rhythmic quality in the appropriateness of plane to quiet length of line, he is able to trace the flowing simplicity of melodious contours of structure as he sees them in what he does to the land itself.*"

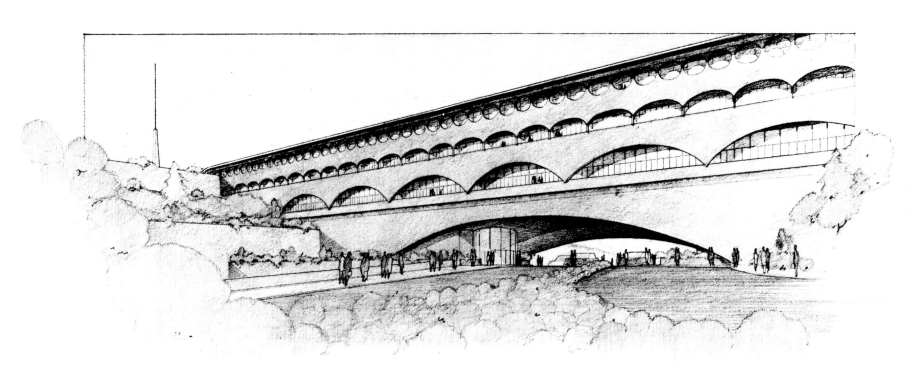

HALL OF JUSTICE

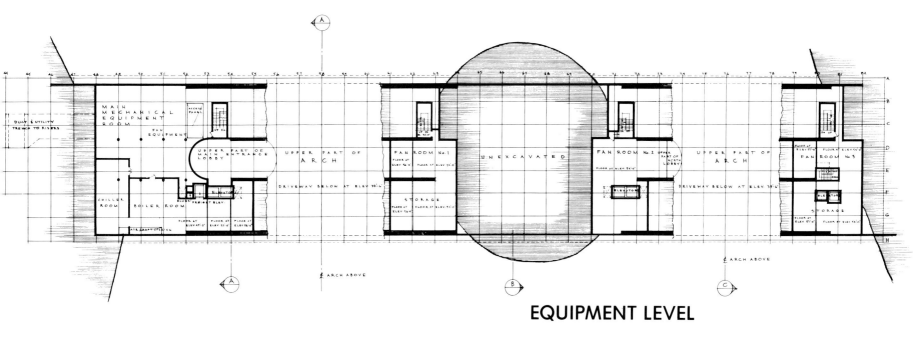

EQUIPMENT LEVEL

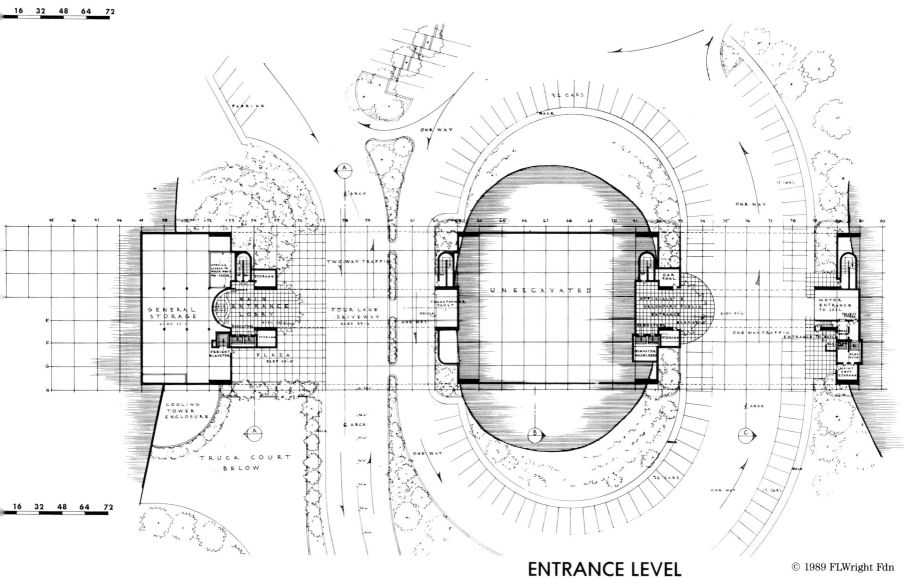

ENTRANCE LEVEL

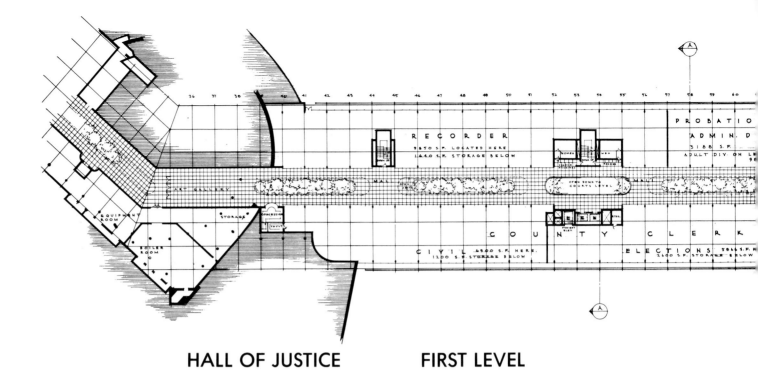

HALL OF JUSTICE   **FIRST LEVEL**

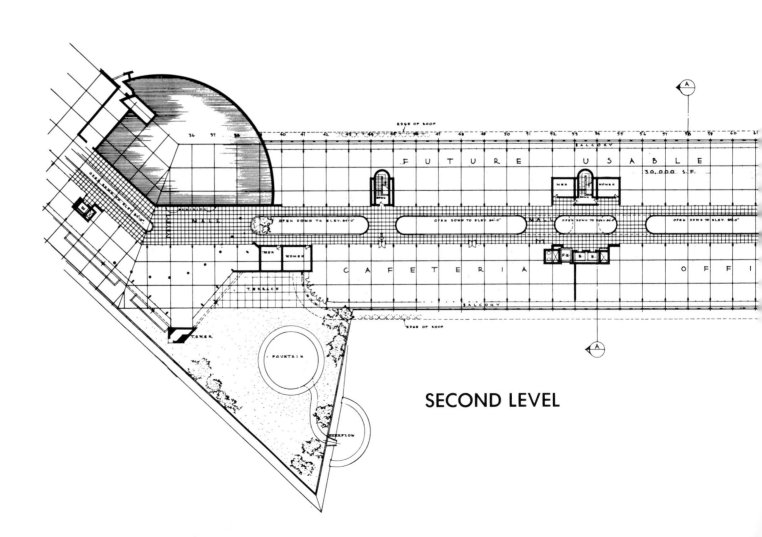

SECOND LEVEL

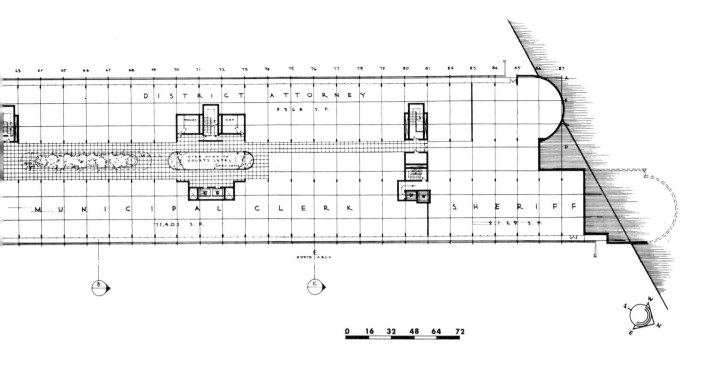

0 16 32 48 64 72

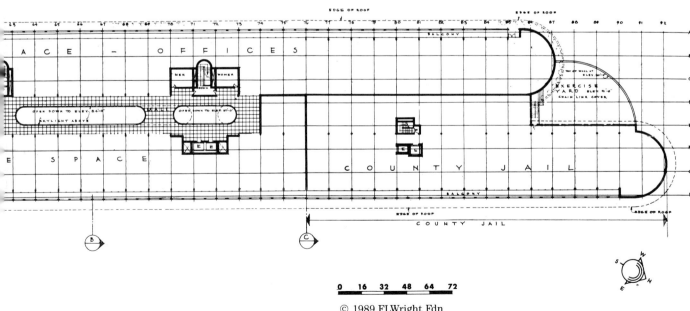

0 16 32 48 64 72

© 1989 FLWright Fdn

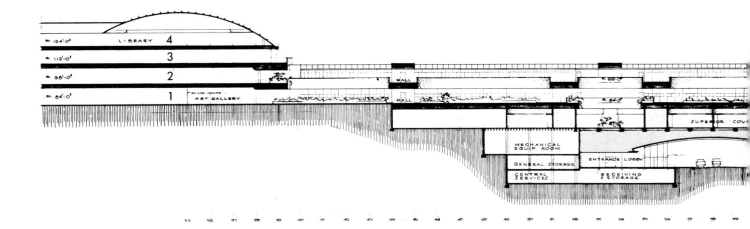

0 16 32 48 64 72

HALL OF JUSTICE

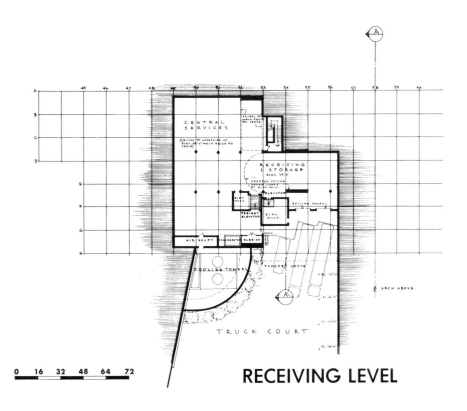

0 16 32 48 64 72

RECEIVING LEVEL

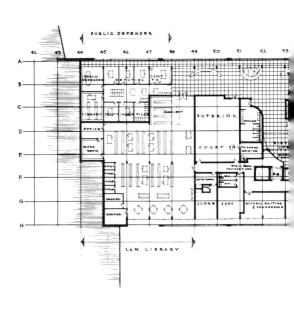

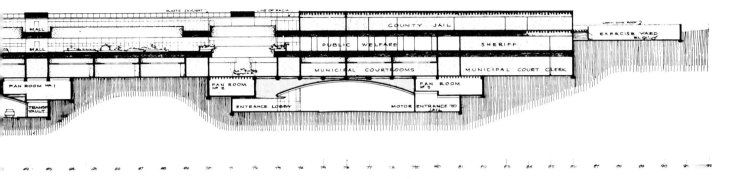

CROSS SECTION

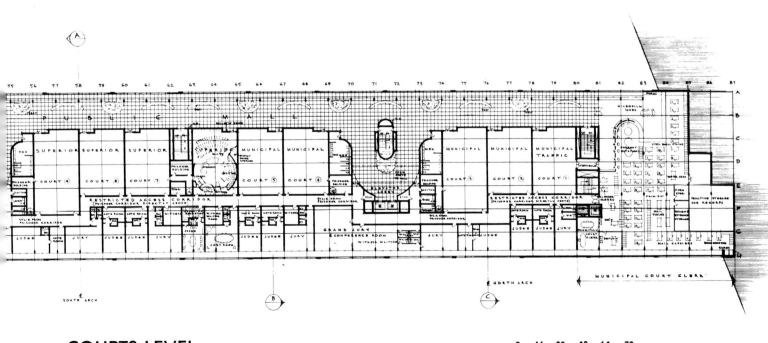

COURTS LEVEL

0 16 32 48 64 72

© 1989 FLWright Fdn

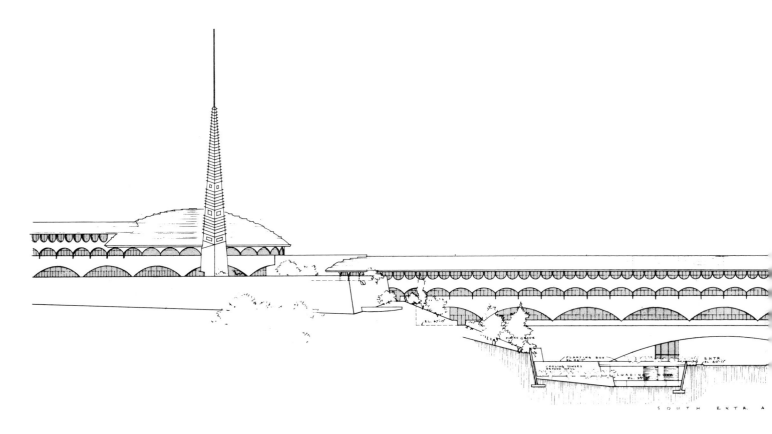

HALL OF JUSTICE

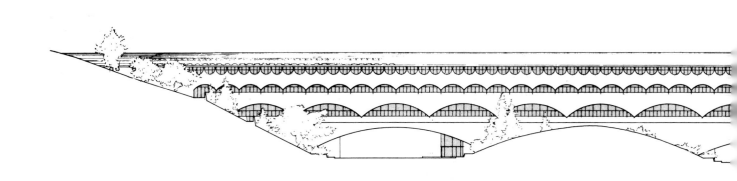

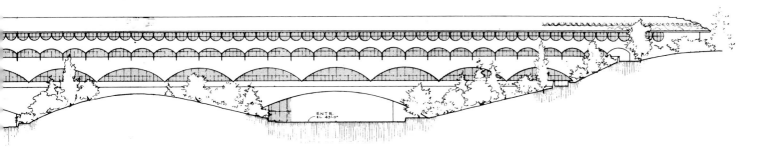

EAST ELEVATION

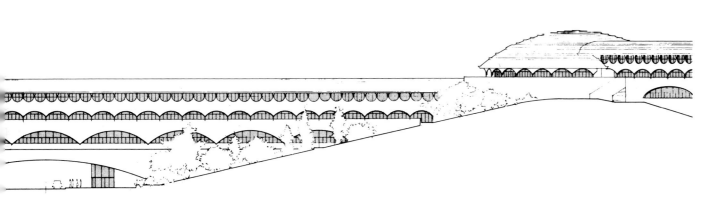

WEST ELEVATION

122

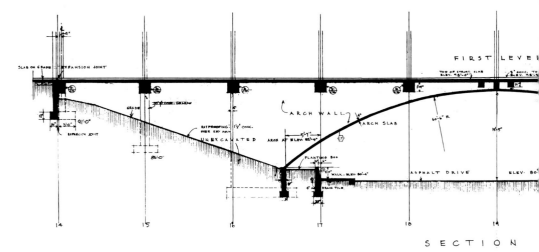

SECTION

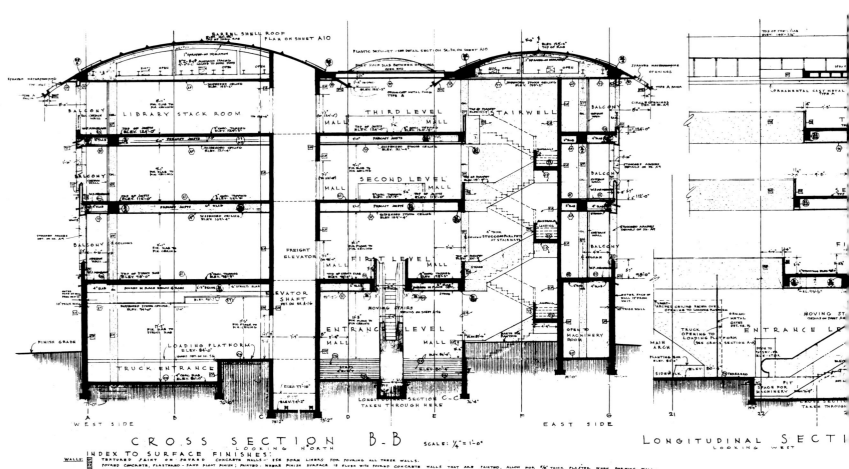

CROSS SECTION B-B
LOOKING NORTH
SCALE: ¼" = 1'-0"

LONGITUDINAL SECTION
LOOKING WEST

INDEX TO SURFACE FINISHES:

WALLS: TEXTURED PAINT ON POURED CONCRETE WALLS - USE FORM LINERS FOR POURING ALL THESE WALLS.
POURED CONCRETE, PLASTERED - SAND FLOAT FINISH; PAINTED. WHERE FINISH SURFACE IS FLUSH WITH POURED CONCRETE WALLS THAT ARE PAINTED, ALLOW FOR ⅝" THICK PLASTER WHEN FORMING WALL.
CEMENT STUCCO - SAND FLOAT FINISH, INTEGRAL COLOR.
½" STUCCO - SAND FLOAT FINISH, INTEGRAL COLOR, OVER POURED CONCRETE.
CONCRETE BLOCK WALLS, PLASTERED - SAND FLOAT FINISH; PAINTED.
GYPSUM PARTITION TILE, PLASTERED - SAND FLOAT FINISH, PAINTED.
TEXTURED PAINT ON DRYWALL PARTITION.
HARDWOOD VENEER PLYWOOD OVER ⅜" PLASTER BOARD ON STUDS.
CERAMIC TILE WAINSCOT 6'-0" HIGH - ABOVE THIS: KEENE'S CEMENT - SAND FLOAT FINISH. PAINTED.
UNFINISHED WALL SURFACES.

FLOORS: ASPHALT TILE.
INTEGRALLY COLORED CONCRETE, STEEL FLOAT FINISH.
CONCRETE, STEEL FLOAT FINISH.
CONCRETE, WOOD FLOAT FINISH.
TERRAZZO.
CERAMIC TILE.

CEILINGS: ACOUSTICAL PLASTER, TEXTURED FINISH, INTEGRAL COLOR.
CEMENT STUCCO - SAND FLOAT FINISH, INTEGRAL COLOR.
UNFINISHED.
KEENE'S CEMENT - SAND FLOAT FINISH, PAINTED.
POURED CONCRETE, TEXTURED PAINT.

OTHER: SITE DEVELOPMENT.
D.F. DRINKING FOUNTAIN.
F.H.C. FIRE HOSE CABINET.

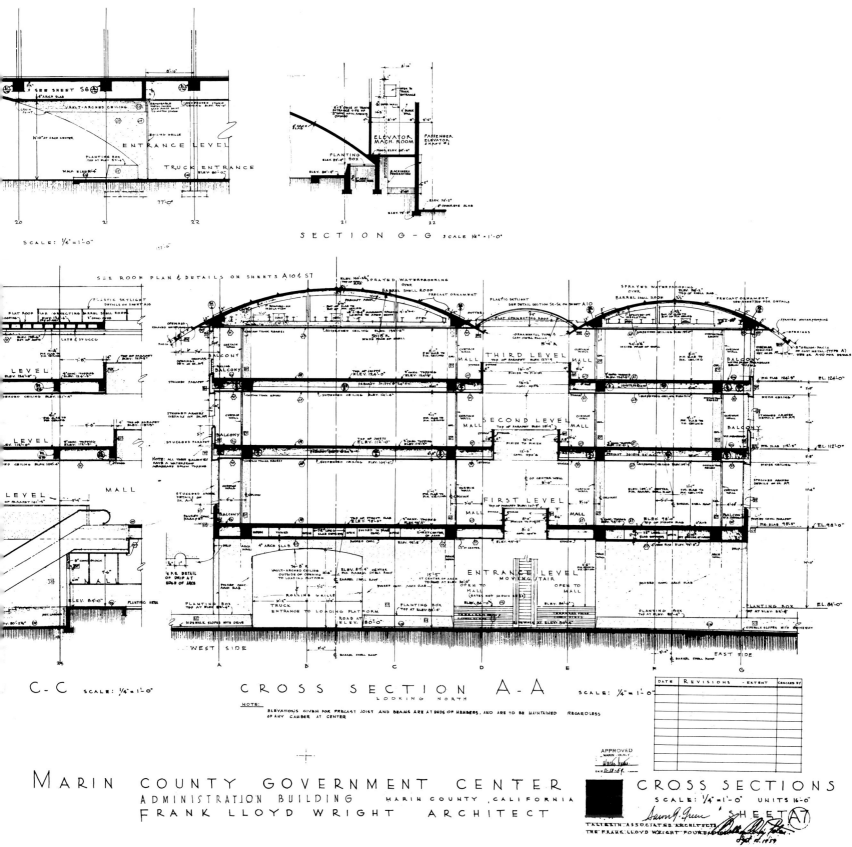

SECTION G-G SCALE 1/4" = 1'-0"

SCALE: 1/4" = 1'-0"

C-C SCALE: 1/4" = 1'-0"

CROSS SECTION A-A
LOOKING NORTH

SCALE: 1/4" = 1'-0"

NOTE:
ELEVATIONS GIVEN FOR PRECAST JOIST AND BEAMS ARE AT ENDS OF MEMBERS, AND ARE TO BE MAINTAINED REGARDLESS OF ANY CAMBER AT CENTER

DATE	REVISIONS — EXTENT	CHECKED BY

APPROVED
MARIN COUNTY

MARIN COUNTY GOVERNMENT CENTER
ADMINISTRATION BUILDING   MARIN COUNTY, CALIFORNIA
FRANK LLOYD WRIGHT   ARCHITECT

CROSS SECTIONS
SCALE: 1/4"=1'-0" UNITS 16'-0"
SHEET A7

TALIESIN ASSOCIATED ARCHITECTS
THE FRANK LLOYD WRIGHT FOUNDATION

© 1989 FLWright Fdn

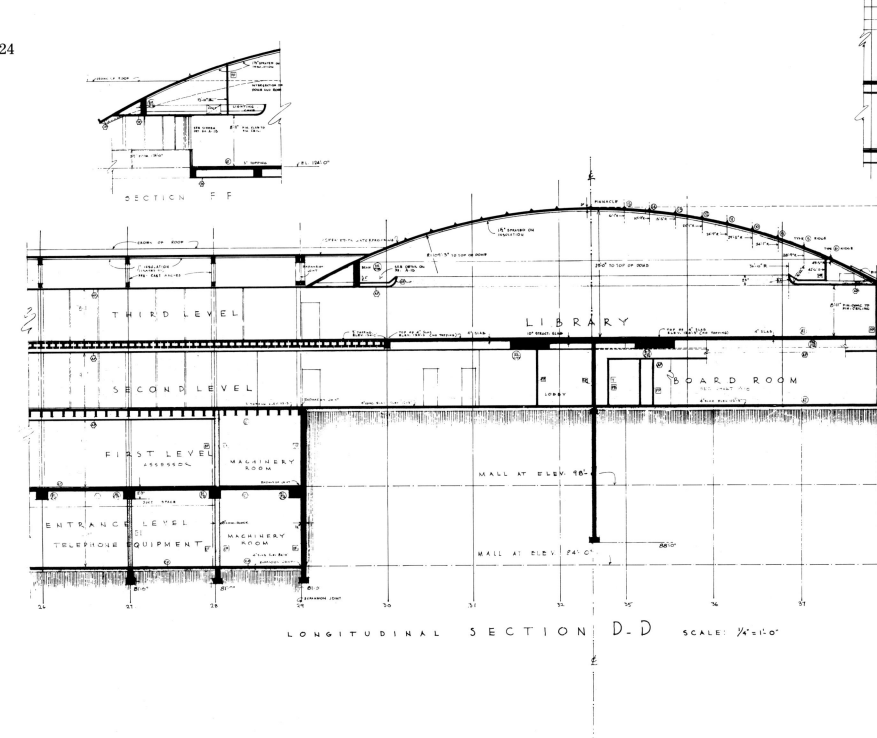

SECTION F F

LONGITUDINAL SECTION D-D SCALE: ¼" = 1'-0"

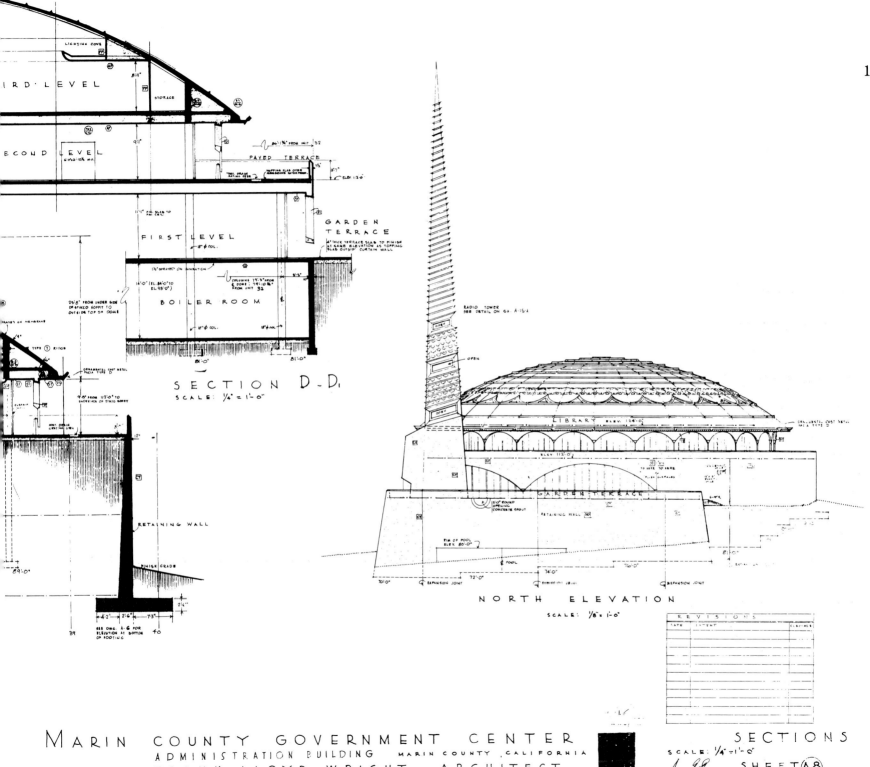

SECTION D - D₁
SCALE: ¼" = 1'-0"

NORTH ELEVATION
SCALE: ⅛" = 1'-0"

RETAINING WALL

MARIN COUNTY GOVERNMENT CENTER
ADMINISTRATION BUILDING   MARIN COUNTY, CALIFORNIA
FRANK LLOYD WRIGHT   ARCHITECT

SECTIONS
SCALE: ¼" = 1'-0"
SHEET A8

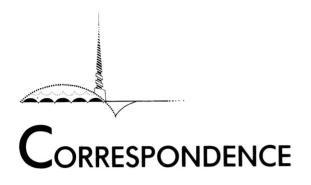

CORRESPONDENCE

PHONE No. 30 3011

TELEGRAMS:
"STATEWORKS, HOBART

ALL COMMUNICATIONS TO BE
ADDRESSED TO THE SECRETARY,
G.P.O. BOX 936J, HOBART

TASMANIA

STT/4

Department of Public Works Tasmania

Hobart 19th. September, 1967

```
WHEN REPLYING
PLEASE QUOTE No.
SEPARATE LETTERS TO BE WRITTEN ON EACH SUBJECT
```

Dear Mr. Green,

      <u>Marin County Hall of Justice.</u>

      Thank you very much for the detailed drawings
of this building. I can see that they will be of great
assistance to us in planning the new Supreme Court buildings
for this State.

               Yours faithfully,

               (S. T. TOMLINSON)
               <u>CHIEF ARCHITECT</u>

SUPREME COURT OF HAWAII
JUDICIARY BUILDING
HONOLULU

CHAMBERS OF
WILLIAM S. RICHARDSON
CHIEF JUSTICE

August 21, 1969

Dear Mr. Green:

      Thank you, again, for showing me the
Marin County court house. The architect for our
court house would like to contact you, or your
group, or the Ford Foundation or American Bar Association group that has designed court houses.

      We're getting close to making our own
plans. Thank you for showing me around. With
kind regards and

      Aloha,

      William S. Richardson

130

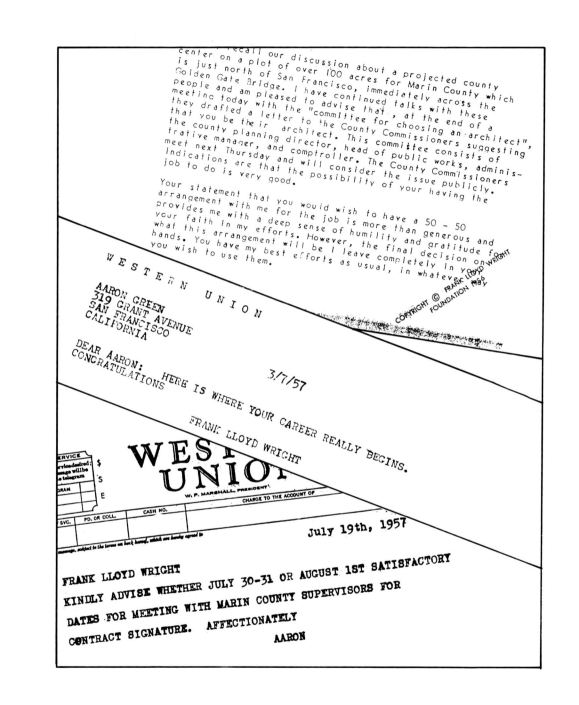

recall our discussion about a projected county center on a plot of over 100 acres for Marin County which is just north of San Francisco, immediately across the Golden Gate Bridge. I have continued talks with these people and am pleased to advise that, at the end of a meeting today with the "committee for choosing an architect", they drafted a letter to the County Commissioners suggesting that you be their architect. This committee consists of the county planning director, head of public works, adminis- trative manager, and comptroller. The County Commissioners meet next Thursday and will consider the issue publicly. Indications are that the possibility of your having the job to do is very good.

Your statement that you would wish to have a 50 - 50 arrangement with me for the job is more than generous and provides me with a deep sense of humility and gratitude for your faith in my efforts. However, the final decision on what this arrangement will be I leave completely in your hands. You have my best efforts as usual, in whatever way you wish to use them.

WESTERN UNION

AARON GREEN
319 GRANT AVENUE
SAN FRANCISCO
CALIFORNIA

3/7/57

DEAR AARON: HERE IS WHERE YOUR CAREER REALLY BEGINS.
CONGRATULATIONS

FRANK LLOYD WRIGHT

WESTERN UNION

W. P. MARSHALL, PRESIDENT

CHARGE TO THE ACCOUNT OF

SVC. PD. OR COLL. CASH NO.

July 19th, 1957

FRANK LLOYD WRIGHT

KINDLY ADVISE WHETHER JULY 30-31 OR AUGUST 1ST SATISFACTORY

DATES FOR MEETING WITH MARIN COUNTY SUPERVISORS FOR

CONTRACT SIGNATURE. AFFECTIONATELY

AARON

December 20, 1973

Dear Aaron,

'Tis a season for fond memories. One of mine
has to do with Mr. Wright and his love for you.

I remember that the three of us were driving
along U.S. 101, having just left the Marin County Civic
Center site where he was to design us a Civic and
Cultural Center. I asked Mr. Wright what your
professional position or relationship with him was.
Mr. Wrights' reply was, "Why, Aaron is my son".
Then looking toward you with great affection in
his voice he repeated, "yes, Aaron is my son."

Your constancy and affectionate dedication to
Frank Lloyd Wright and his work doubtless brought
forth this his greatest gift to you—"you are my son."

Have a Merry Christmas!

Affectionately
Mary Summers

世 Peace on Earth

界 Paix sur la Terre

和 Paz en la Tierra

平 Мир на Земле

APPENDIX

PHOTOGRAPHY CREDITS

Front Cover: © 1989 Monte Madeiros, all rights reserved
Back Cover: © 1989 Steven Henneman, all rights reserved (First Place, "Focus on Frank Lloyd Wright"
Photography Competition)

P. 3	Pedro E. Guerrero
P. 21	*Oakland Tribune*
P. 26-27	John Amarantides, courtesy of the Frank Lloyd Wright Foundation
P. 29	R. E. Campbell
P. 30	Jan Novie (2)
P. 31	Jan Novie (3)
P. 32	Jan Novie
P. 33	Karl Riek
P. 34	Karl Riek
P. 35	Karl Riek
P. 36	Jan Novie (2)
P. 37	Jan Novie (*top*), William Schwarz
P. 38	Jan Novie (4)
P. 39	Monte Madeiros
P. 40	© 1989 Leanne Maas, all rights reserved
P. 41	Jan Novie
P. 46	Jan Novie
P. 47	© 1989 Brian P. Boas, all rights reserved
P. 48	Aaron G. Green, courtesy of the National Center for the Study of Frank Lloyd Wright
P. 50	Karl Riek
P. 51	*Marin Independent Journal*, reprinted, by permission
P. 52	Karl Riek
P. 53	John Amarantides, courtesy of the Frank Lloyd Wright Foundation
P. 54	Valerie Johnson
P. 56	Valerie Johnson
P. 57	John Amarantides, courtesy of the Frank Lloyd Wright Foundation
P. 58	Jan Novie (3)
P. 59	Jan Novie
P. 60	Karl Riek
P. 61	Karl Riek
P. 62	Photographer unknown
P. 72	Karl Riek (2)
P. 79	Aaron G. Green (*top*), Karl Riek
P. 84	Reprinted from the Frank Lloyd Wright *Square Paper*
P. 86	Aaron G. Green (*left*, 2); *Marin Independent Journal*, reprinted, by permission (2)
P. 87	*Marin Independent Journal*, reprinted, by permission (4)
P. 93	Jan Novie (2)
P. 103	Jan Novie (2)
P. 109	*Marin Independent Journal*, reprinted, by permission

LOUIS SULLIVAN ON FRANK LLOYD WRIGHT

Ben Raeburn comments on Louis Sullivan's writings about Frank Lloyd Wright and his seismic design of the Imperial Hotel.

It was 1885. At the age of eighteen, Frank Lloyd Wright made some drawings to apply for a job with Louis Sullivan, the man he eventually came to regard as his "beloved master." Mr. Sullivan looked at the drawings and he said, "You've got the right kind of touch. You'll do."

In the years following, Mr. Wright had created, before 1910, some of America's greatest architecture, among them the Larkin Building, Unity Temple, the Willits House, the Coonley House, the Robie House.

In the early Twenties, he had finished his most important building worldwide, the Imperial Hotel in Tokyo, Japan. The world could not know that the Imperial was destined to ride out the disastrous 1923 earthquake in Tokyo unharmed, housing and caring for hundreds of homeless families while the city lay about it in ruins.

Louis Sullivan, many years before, had understood the startling potential of his gifted pupil, had in later years perceived the humanity involved in Frank Lloyd Wright's organic concepts, and had understood his depth of insight into the future for architecture, for the insightful architect in the perennial future.

The following brief excerpts from Louis Sullivan's insights into the perceptions of Frank Lloyd Wright will confirm their permanent importance:

> "It is in this sense that we are now about to contemplate the new Imperial Hotel in Tokyo, Japan.

> "This great work is the masterpiece of Frank Lloyd Wright, a great free spirit, whose fame as a master of ideas is an accomplished world-wide fact.

> "Through prior visits he had discerned, and added to the wealth of his own rich nature, the spirit, as evidenced in forms of the ideals of Old Japan, which still persist, in slumber, among its living people, needing but the awakening touch.

> "It is a high faculty of what we call genius to penetrate and temporarily to reside within the genius of another people foreign to our own local ways. And it is this quality of vision, this receptivity, this openness of mind, that especially signalizes the free spirit — the mind free from provincialism and the fear of life.

"Next in order to the power of vision comes the power to interpret in thought; and, next to this, the power to express the thought, the state of feeling in concrete terms.

"In this structure is not to be found a single form distinctly Japanese; nor that of any other country; yet in its own individual form, its mass, and subsidiaries, its evolution of plan and development of thesis; in its sedulous care for niceties of administration, and for the human sense of joy, it has expressed, in inspiring form as an epic poem, addressed to the Japanese people, their inmost thought. It is characterized by the quality, *Shibui*, a Japanese word, signifying the reward of earnest contemplation. In studying the concrete expression, the embodiment of idea in solid form, the magnitude of this structure should always be borne in mind. It is 300 × 500 feet on the ground, the area thus equaling 150,000 square feet, or nearly two and one-half times the area covered by the great Auditorium Building in Chicago. The structure is three stories high in the main, with special masses equivalent in height to seven stories.

"In a sense it is a huge association of structures, a gathering of the clans, so to speak; it is a seeming aggregate of buildings shielding beauteous gardens, sequestered among them.

"The general construction of the building is definitely based upon the reinforced-concrete-slab idea, carried out by the architect theoretically and practically to its limits, in a manner so novel, so logical, so convincing, as to be of the highest technical interest to those familiar with the general slab idea. The specific application here has to do directly with a flexible resistance to earth-quakes — developing shocks, undulations, oscillations, and twists, in action.

"The entire structure thus rests upon a flexible foundation which is free to yield to the mutations of earthquake disturbance and come back to place again.

"This structure, designed theoretically and worked out practically to withstand distortion or fracture by earthquake, was put to the test while nearing completion in April, 1922, in broad daylight, during the heaviest temblor in point of severity Japan had known in fifty years. Wide destruction was wrought in the city of Tokyo. The shock was terrific. The Imperial was violently jolted. It visibly trembled, swayed and rocked in the upheaval, and at its ending quietly steadied to position, free of distortion, rents or damage of any kind.

"So much for a system of construction altogether novel in conception and execution, carried out by a strong, persistent mind, as imaginative in its insight into fundamental principles of engineering as in its profound insight into the romance of breathing life and beauty, humanity and spirit, into forms and materials otherwise helplessly inert.

"In planning the erection of a structure in a terrain habitually given to earthquake it would seem to be natural to regard earthquake — otherwise seismic disturbance — as a fundamental. For earthquakes are not imaginary or abstract or illusory; they are real — and at times calamitous.

"It is precisely this power of the poet to bring earthquake vividly into consciousness and hold it there, that distinguishes him, in this instance, from the unispired engineer. The latter is an extremely useful person, wherever and whenever his formulas, his slide-rule, his tables and his precedents — to which he is a slave — apply. Within the limits of routine he may successfully vary his processes in application; and there his social value ends. The same, in substance, may be said of the uninspired practicing architect, except that the latter, in addition, is invertebrate. Wherever he thinks with reasonable clearness, he approaches the engineer; but he is not a Yea-Sayer — he prefers to trim. Yet the great creative engineer — and there have been such — by virtue of clear eyesight, material realization and the power to dream, is again the poet if he fail not in the human sense of beauty, even though he may not think so, and out of prudence may not say so.

"The emergence, unharmed, of the Imperial Hotel, from the heart-rending horrors of the Tokyo disaster, takes on, at once, momentous importance in the world of modern thought, as a triumph of the living and the real over the credulous, the fantastic and the insane."

After Sullivan learned that the Imperial had withstood the earthquake, he undertook to write an article for the *Record*, in which this sentence appears "…This most significant architectural monument that the modern world can show stands today uninjured because it was thought-built."

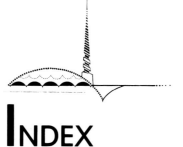

INDEX